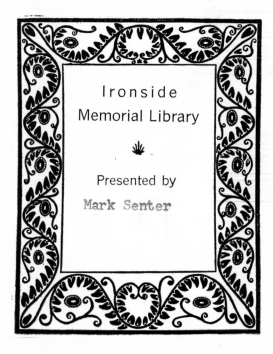

THE HISTORIC CHURCH
AND MODERN PACIFISM

THE HISTORIC CHURCH AND MODERN PACIFISM

By

UMPHREY LEE

ABINGDON-COKESBURY PRESS

New York • *Nashville*

THE HISTORIC CHURCH AND MODERN PACIFISM
COPYRIGHT, MCMXLIII
By WHITMORE & STONE

THIS BOOK HAS BEEN MANUFACTURED IN COMPLI-
ANCE WITH ORDERS OF THE WAR PRODUCTION BOARD
FOR CONSERVING PAPER AND OTHER MATERIALS

SET UP, PRINTED, AND BOUND BY THE
PARTHENON PRESS AT NASHVILLE, TEN-
NESSEE, UNITED STATES OF AMERICA

25445

To
JOHN WHITEHURST
a good soldier in every warfare

ACKNOWLEDGMENTS

To record the thought of the Christian Church on any subject through two thousand years of history is, of course, an impossible task. In such a brief survey as this much has been omitted, and there will inevitably be differences of opinion concerning the selection of materials as well as concerning interpretation of them. The Notes will indicate the works quoted in the text and some collateral material, but they in no way constitute a bibliography of the Church and War. The reader will doubtless recognize the author's indebtedness to many scholars unnamed.

Scriptural quotations in this volume are from the American Standard Version of the Revised Bible, copyright renewal, 1929, the International Council of Religious Education, owner, and are used by permission.

For the third time I am indebted to Mrs. Dallas E. Hawkins for help in the preparation of a manuscript for the press. My wife has again assisted me in many ways, including the drudgery of reading proof.

UMPHREY LEE

Southern Methodist University

7

Table of Contents

INTRODUCTION

THE JUSTIFICATION OF THE PRESENT WORK IS IN certain apparently widespread misconceptions about the position of the historic Church on the question which Luther phrased, "Can the soldier also be saved?" It seems, for example, to be rather commonly believed that until the time of Constantine the Church was consistently pacifist, and that after Constantine the Church became militarist because of compromises for political reasons. This is believed in spite of specific studies made by the greatest of modern church historians, Adolf Harnack, A. C. McGiffert, and James Moffatt. There are other misconceptions about what Christian thinkers have actually said about war and about the duty of Christians. Moreover, it seems to be taken for granted by some that the question of the Christian's attitude toward war can be studied apart from his relation to the State and to the social order. If this short work has a good deal to say about the State, about courts, about the family, even about property, it is because the subjects cannot be ignored by those who would understand the Church's attitude toward the soldier. There is, of course, no attempt to write the history of Christian doctrines of the State; the reader must look elsewhere for this.[1] The only purpose is to sketch briefly the history of the Church's position in regard to war and against this background to consider "modern pacifism."

There are other reasons for this book. Every age tends to think of itself as having discovered truth which former times did not know or had forgotten. But even Sappho was not the first to call beauty, beauty. Most of the ethical questions which trouble Christians today were, in their essence, considered by Christians of former times. And this is especially true of the problem of war and peace. Certainly, the leaders of historic Christendom were not doddering old gentlemen eager to barter their heritage for political pottage.

If modern historical studies have taught us anything, it is that a movement like Christianity can be understood only in the light of what it has been. The past can be discarded, but only after it has been examined and appraised. This study is concerned, not with the acts of the Church, but with what it said. It is an essay in the history of the Christian witness. Not all Christians have said the same things, but there is a unity as well as a diversity. When we have become aware of this unity and of this diversity, perhaps we can better understand and judge the sentiments of Christians today.

The writer has not tried to set forth the facts under the pretense that he has no opinions of his own; but he believes that there is here no distortion of the sources. On the whole, the conclusions are supported by competent historians whose words are accepted by scholars the world over. The work is intended for everyone who may be interested in the question of the Christian soldier and not simply for scholars or church historians. But the latter will find references to the authorities and especially to the sources in the Notes.

homiletical rather than critical. In considering the sayings of Jesus as they bear upon war, no purpose would be served by reviewing the almost innumerable books and articles which have been published, especially in this country, to establish the pacifism of Jesus. It will suffice to follow the arguments of reputable scholars who have both the historical training and the disposition to deal with a complex and by no means easy subject.

Among the writers on the attitude of the New Testament and the Early Church toward war who have concluded that Jesus can be interpreted only from the pacifist position, perhaps the most thoughtful and thorough is Professor C. J. Cadoux. In a book entitled *The Early Church and the World*,[2] Professor Cadoux has studied the whole subject of the Early Church's attitude toward the society of which it was a part; and concerning war he has incorporated, with some additions, the findings of an earlier book, *The Early Christian Attitude Toward War*. The volume first mentioned, published in 1925, is one of the best historical justifications of the pacifist position.[3] Our method here will be to consider the passages which the author considers proof of Jesus' pacifism.

Quite rightly, Professor Cadoux dismisses those references of Jesus to war which are simply illustrative allusions. When he said, "I came not to send peace, but a sword," he was obviously using figurative language with no thought of approving literal swords. When he told of kings preparing for war he had no intention of recommending their example as state policy. The story of the centurion in whom Jesus found more faith than in all Israel is perhaps less easily dismissed, since Jesus had such an admirable opportunity to point out the impossibility of maintaining a righteous life and serving in the army. On the whole, however, Cadoux is possibly right in insisting that Jesus was here dealing with a stranger and a Gentile and was not speaking of his moral character.

According to Cadoux, there are some specific statements of Jesus concerning war. The first of these is found in Matthew 24:15-22.

When therefore ye see the abomination of desolation, which was spoken of through Daniel the prophet, standing in the holy place (let him that readeth understand), then let them that are in Judaea flee unto the mountains: let him that is on the housetop not go down to take out the things that are in his house: and let him that is in the field not return back to take his cloak. But woe unto them that are with child and to them that give suck in those days! And pray ye that your flight be not in the winter, neither on a sabbath: for then shall be great tribulation, such as hath not been from the beginning of the world until now, no, nor ever shall be. And except those days had been shortened, no flesh would have been saved: but for the elect's sake those days shall be shortened.

According to the interpretation proposed by Cadoux, Jesus here bids his disciples flee from Jerusalem when the Roman armies come to besiege it in A.D. 70, and thereby makes clear that he does not approve even of a defensive war.

The use of this passage as a specific instruction of Jesus concerning war is, to say the least, startling.

It ignores completely the words with which the passage begins in both Matthew and Mark. Matthew has the disciples on the Mount of Olives asking: "Tell us, when shall these things be? and what shall be the sign of thy coming, and of the end of the world?" Mark says that Peter, James, John, and Andrew on the Mount of Olives asked: "Tell us, when shall these things be? and what shall be the sign when these things are all about to be accomplished?" Mark and Matthew both refer to the appearance of the false Messiah, the Antichrist of Apocalyptic literature. Both speak of wars and rumors of wars, of famines and earthquakes. Both speak of a great tribulation. Both refer to the "abomination of desolation," a phrase also familiar in the Apocalyptic literature. All these— the appearance of Antichrist, the Great Tribulation, the Flight of Believers—are signs of the End in the Apocalyptic books; and all these appear in the account in Matthew and Mark.

This passage as a whole refers to the End of the Age, and has been traditionally so interpreted by the Church. Modern scholars have tended to question the section because it seems to incorporate material of different kinds. For instance, Canon Charles and a number of others think that it is a Christian adaptation of an originally Jewish work written in A.D. 67-68 during the period just preceding the Fall of Jerusalem.[4] I have no brief for this view, but the reasons for it are instructive. One of the principal ones is that Christ frequently speaks of his Coming in connection with his death and resurrection (Matt. 10:23; Mark

9:1; 14:62), but always speaks of the Fall of Jerusalem by itself. For example, when he wept over the city, saying, "If thou hadst known . . . . the things which belong unto thy peace," he spoke of a time when enemies would cast a trench about Jerusalem and besiege it on every side, and leave not one stone upon another. But he did not connect this with his Second Coming. (Luke 19:41-44.) And, incidentally, neither here nor in the later passage, Luke 23:28-30, does he say anything about nonresistance.

In the passage in Mark 13 and the similar sections of Matthew there is an apparent reference to the Fall of Jerusalem. In trying to guess why this has been picked upon as a key passage to show that Jesus disapproved of even a defensive war, one may suppose that a short reference in the church historian Eusebius, who died about A.D. 340, is responsible. Eusebius says that "The whole body, however, of the church at Jerusalem, having been commanded by a divine revelation, given to men of approved piety there before the war, removed from the city, and dwelt at a certain town beyond the Jordan, called Pella." [5] The Christians did flee Jerusalem. But they fled, not to the mountains, as they certainly would have done if they had thought that Jesus had commanded them to do so, but to a city across Jordan hated by the Jews, a town that they would not have chosen except for safety.[6] So far as I know there is no reference to this flight except in Eusebius, and there it is distinctly said that the Christians acted in response to a revelation that some of their worthy men had just before

22

the war. In other words, the Christians in Jerusalem at the time of the Fall did not think that they had any command from Jesus concerning their conduct. They sought refuge from the destruction which they saw would be the result of the insane rebellion.

To get back to the passage which Cadoux considers a specific instruction concerning war: there is a vague reference to the destruction of Jerusalem embodied in a discourse on the End of the Age. The Flight of the Believers is a part of the Apocalyptic pattern, and the Christians at the time of the Fall of Jerusalem never thought to connect it with their own situation. In short, the passage can be made to enjoin a policy of nonresistance only by an exegesis that neither conforms to traditional interpretation nor takes account of modern scholarship.

The second specific instruction, according to Cadoux, is that addressed to Peter in the Garden. "Put up again thy sword into its place: for all they that take the sword shall perish with the sword." (Matt. 26:52.) The circumstances of this prohibition are admittedly special, but Cadoux thinks that the "grim truth" on which the prohibition is founded is general. He would agree with Tertullian that, in disarming Peter, the Lord had unbelted every soldier.

However, it should perhaps be noted for the record that this saying is recorded only by Matthew. Again, the quotation above is not all that Jesus is reported to have said to Peter. The full quotation is: "Put up again thy sword into its place: for all they that take the sword shall perish with the sword. Or

23

thinkest thou that I cannot beseech my Father, and he shall even now send me more than twelve legions of angels? How then should the scriptures be fulfilled, that thus it must be?" Unless we are to rule out all but the proverblike saying of Jesus, "for all they that take the sword," the plain meaning of the passage is that Jesus had the angelic hosts at his command, but his appointed way was to die according to the Scriptures.

But he said, "they that take the sword shall perish with the sword." Undoubtedly, he meant just what he said. It is a commonplace of moralists that violence begets violence. The form is common with Jesus. "Judge not, that ye be not judged"; "He that is not against you is for you." But one must remember that the proverbial form is always used for a particular purpose without care to insure application in every other instance. Bishop Gore's warning must always be heeded in interpreting the sayings of Jesus. "Proverbs," he wrote once, "are principles stated in extremes, without modification, often requiring to be balanced by their seeming contraries." [7]

Jesus, therefore, replied to Peter that force was not to be used, although he had at his command the angelic hosts if they were needed. He couched his words partly in proverbial form, emphasizing the well-known truth that violence would lead only to violence, the sword to death. If the unhappy zeal of Peter had been a violation of the cardinal ethical tenet of Jesus, it might have been expected that he would have administered a far severer rebuke, and the rebuke itself would not have been forgotten by the other two Synoptists, Mark and Luke. If Jesus chose this as the time to utter a thorough prohibition of all participation in armed conflict and chose to do this by the declaration that those who take the sword will perish by it, he could hardly have chosen a worse time to enforce the lesson. Jesus did not resist, but in a few hours he was crucified.

Looked at in any way, it seems more reasonable to take the plain meaning of the words. Jesus ordered Peter to cease resistance. He insisted that if he needed help of that kind, he could have it from heaven. And he enforced his prohibition by reminding Peter that resistance only meant death for the disciples; violence begets violence. Understood in this way, the words preserved by Matthew make sense. No one will deny the "grim truth" which they express, but to quote them as a statement of pacifism is to do violence to their plain meaning.

The third passage which Cadoux quotes as a specific reference to war is the temptation in which Jesus refused to worship the devil.

Again, the devil taketh him unto an exceeding high mountain, and showeth him all the kingdoms of the world, and the glory of them; and he said unto him, All these things will I give thee, if thou wilt fall down and worship me. Then saith Jesus unto him, Get thee hence, Satan: for it is written, Thou shalt worship the Lord thy God, and him only shalt thou serve. (Matt. 4:8-10.)

According to the interpretation of Cadoux, Jesus knew that the most practical way to secure dominion over all the kingdoms of the world was by force, and in rejecting the temptation of the devil he declared his opposition to coercive methods.

Jesus' Kingdom was not of this world. His disciples were not to act as the rulers of the Gentiles who lorded it over their followers: they were to be men of humility, of forgiveness and love. But in making this temptation a specific renunciation of war, Cadoux and others who adopt this interpretation show the influence of recent attempts to explain Jesus and his message in terms of the political situation in Palestine. It will help to look more closely at this interpretation.

Professor Simkhovitch popularized this emphasis upon the tension between Jewish nationalism and Roman rule.[8] The argument is that Jesus, aware of this tension and feeling the impulse of Jewish patriotism, resolved the conflict by deliberately preaching a kingdom of inward righteousness, of humility and love. He did not renounce the national aspirations of his people because of prudence, a belief that rebellion against the Romans would be futile, but through conscious acceptance of the situation. He met force with love. According to Simkhovitch, the temptation to worship the devil and secure the kingdoms of this world was a temptation to accept the Romanization of his people. The temptation to cast himself down from the Temple pinnacle was to throw in his lot with the Zealots, who were the revolutionary party.

Older scholars undoubtedly ignored the problem

of Roman rule in first-century Palestine; but later writers have made too much of it. Jesus stood in the line of prophets and sages; he was the heir of a great and ancient religious tradition. To explain his message in terms of contemporary Palestinian politics is an unwarrantable narrowing of him and of his meaning for the world.

Moreover, in attempting to draw modern parallels and find lessons for our times, the actual picture of the first century is easily distorted. Only recently, for example, a writer on "The New Testament and War and Peace" thus presented the Zealots. "This point of view, it may be observed, is that of the majority of Christians and non-Christians today, who believe that one has the right, nay the duty, to take up arms in defense of national rights, liberty, and religious faith." [9] In other words, the Zealots were simply Jews who believed that one should resist the Romans in behalf of Jewish rights and liberties. But who really were the Zealots?

The Zealots arose as a protest party against the nonpolitical attitude of the Pharisees. They were indeed in part a product of persecution, but they were not merely a group of patriot Jews who differed from their countrymen only in the doctrine of resistance. They were, in Fairweather's phrases, "a fanatical war party," "simply fanatical extremists." They held to a Messianic hope, but "the attitude taken up by them was thoroughly antagonistic to that hope [that is, the true Messianic doctrine], which is founded upon the conception of an ideal and invisible kingdom. . . ." [10] Herford believes that the Apocalyptic literature of the period just before the time of Christ is Zealot literature. These writings

showed the future bliss of the righteous and the torments of the wicked, and drew both pictures in bold lines and glaring colours. They were full of religious zeal, but it was the religion of fanatics, in which sincere piety was allied to hatred, and the sacred consciousness of being the chosen people of God became a bitter national pride—blind, fierce and cruel.[11]

This literature and the Zealot movement, contends Herford, went hand in hand.

Whether Herford's theory concerning the Apocalyptic literature be correct or not, there is common agreement among scholars as to the fanatical character of the Zealot movement. To represent them, therefore, as simply those Jews who believed that resistance to oppression is sometimes justified is bad history, to say nothing more. The truth is that in Jesus' day most Jews found a *via media* between the self-seeking of certain money-makers and the fanaticism of the Zealots. John has preserved a story in which the Jews indignantly deny that they had ever been in bondage to any man (John 8:33), which may very well have represented the attitude of many of the contemporaries of Jesus. Their political position was so little in their thoughts that they even denied their subjection.

Above all, we must not modernize the picture. In Jesus' day only the very, very few had anything to say about the way in which they were governed. The

28

masses the world over not only had nothing to say about their government; most of them probably knew little about it. It was not only in Palestine that people lived out their lives under foreign domination. And to most of them it made little difference whether their rulers were of their own people or foreigners.[12] In dealing, therefore, with the problems of Jesus' world, we must not read into that situation questions of interventionism and isolationism, of peace and war, as they are known today, when in some countries, at least, men cast their ballots to determine national action. Jesus lived in the first century. It may be legitimate to believe that he spoke for the twentieth century; but it is certainly not legitimate to compare ordinary citizens who do not want to fight, but who believe that there are circumstances in which it would be justified, with wild fanatics of the first century who believed themselves divinely ordained to wade through blood to the domination of the world by a chosen nation.

There are, then, grave reasons for questioning the interpretation of the Temptation in terms of the conflict between Jewish nationalism and the Roman power. But if this were admitted, it would be a long cry from the rejection of the rebellious program of the Zealots to a pronouncement upon the conduct of Christians in a twentieth-century war.

The saying of Jesus most often quoted as the authorization of pacifism is Matthew 5:38-41.

Ye have heard that it was said, An eye for an eye, and a tooth for a tooth: but I say unto you, Resist not him that is

29

evil: but whosoever smiteth thee on thy right cheek, turn to him the other also. And if any man would go to law with thee, and take away thy coat, let him have thy cloak also. And whosoever shall compel thee to go one mile, go with him two.

Professor Cadoux does not quote this as one of the "pertinent specific instructions" concerning war, an omission that might surprise readers accustomed to the homiletical hospitality of many writers on the subject. According to Cadoux, this passage forbids "not merely the indulgence of personal resentment, but also the infliction of judicial penalties." [13]

It should be obvious that Cadoux is not minimizing the evidence for the pacifist position; he is not trying to "emasculate the gospel." As a conscientious scholar he recognizes that Jesus is not here referring to war. He argues that the doctrine of "an eye for an eye" was a provision of public justice, and for this Jesus meant to substitute the "duty of neighbourly love." If this is correct, any literal following of Jesus would mean the refusal of Christians to sanction any judicial system with which we are now familiar.

The passage merits the close examination which has been given to it by commentators of all shades of belief. Mr. A. T. Cadoux—who is not to be confused with Professor C. J. Cadoux—notes that Jesus illustrates his injunction to resist not evil by three examples: turning the other cheek, giving up one's cloak, and going the second mile. In all three cases the class of injury is the same, and the conduct enjoined is not merely nonresistance, but the supplying of the evildoer "with more of what he seeks by his evil deed."

He who would strike you on one cheek is to have another opportunity to strike; he who would take your coat is to have your cloak also; he who would compel you to go one mile is to have you for the second. And no third person is involved. The only sufferer is the one who is enjoined to satisfy the demands of the evildoer.[14]

Professor James Moffatt has an interesting comment on the injunction to turn the other cheek. Fifteen hundred years ago Augustine had been bothered by the words, "whosoever smiteth thee on thy right cheek." A right-handed man would not ordinarily smite another on the *right* cheek. Moffatt remarks that the reference is obviously to a blow delivered with the back of the hand, an insult rather than an injury.[15] Certainly, this kind of blow would be similar to the other misdeeds. Neither the taking of one's coat nor impressment for a mile would incapacitate the sufferer. And in each instance, only the one is injured.

These are not quibbles, but honest efforts to arrive at Jesus' meaning. It is noteworthy that those who are interested in establishing the doctrine of universal nonresistance do not usually mention the verse which follows Matthew 5:38-41, that is, verse 42: "Give to him that asketh thee, and from him that would borrow of thee turn not thou away." Luke gives these sayings in another setting which does not mention nonresistance and the statement about "an eye for an eye." In Luke's version the passage reads as follows:

But I say unto you that hear, Love your enemies, do good to them that hate you, bless them that curse you, pray for them that despitefully use you. To him that smiteth thee on the one cheek offer also the other; and from him that taketh away thy cloak withhold not thy coat also. Give to every one that asketh thee; and of him that taketh away thy goods ask them not again. And as ye would that men should do to you, do ye also to them likewise. (Luke 6:27-31.)

The interpreter of Jesus, if he chooses, may understand that the provisions of these passages, as recorded in Matthew and Luke, command nonresistance under all circumstances; but there is no critical authority for such an interpretation. If there is in this famous exhortation of Jesus any reference wider than that of personal attitudes to private injuries, it is unquestionably, as Cadoux insists, to judicial sentences. But, in the light of the context of the sayings in Matthew and Luke, it would seem that the words of Jesus here refer to the individual's personal reaction to injuries, forbidding the exaction of private vengeance and exhorting to positive good will.

Professor G. H. C. MacGregor has made a thorough study of the New Testament teaching concerning war in his book, *The New Testament Basis of Pacifism*. He depends for his principal argument upon "certain basic principles of the Christian ethic as set forth in Jesus' teaching and illustrated by his example." These principles are: (1) love toward one's neighbors; (2) belief in a Father God who loves all men impartially and sets an infinite value on every individual human soul; and (3) Jesus' way of life, above all, the Cross.[16] This is an entirely legitimate and potent method of argument, but it is theological and not exegetical. This procedure would seem to be by far the most reasonable approach to the whole question; but to deduce from theological principles the course of conduct obligatory upon Christians, while legitimate and even necessary, is not an exposition of Jesus' teaching concerning war. And Professor MacGregor himself is not content to rest his case here.

In dealing with the obvious question, Where does Jesus justify this extension of his teaching to cover the question of war? MacGregor declares that Jesus consciously applied his teaching to the problem of war in refusing to wage a Messianic crusade. ". . . . So far as we can see, the refusal of Jesus to wage war as Messiah was due first and foremost to the fact that . . . . He regarded the war-method as inherently evil, a violation of His own supreme command to love one's neighbor as oneself. . . . "[17]

This, of course, is simply to repeat the argument of Cadoux concerning the Temptation of Jesus, and nothing more needs to be said about it here. The fact is that none of the statements cited as specific instructions concerning war either by Cadoux or MacGregor can be justified as such except by complicated, if ingenious, reasoning. The simple truth would seem to be that Jesus left no statement on the question, at least none which has been preserved in the Gospels. This is not surprising when one remembers that he also left, for example, no statement concerning the institution of private property. It may be well to look more closely at this problem.

Cadoux thinks that Jesus did express relative approval of private property when he said that "your heavenly Father knoweth that ye have need of all these things." But an acknowledgment of man's need for food and clothing by no means indicates approval of private ownership. It is only another evidence of our insistence upon reading into Jesus' words what we think he should have said. It is true that Jesus probably owned the carpenter shop in Nazareth after Joseph's death, but we do not know this. He denounced greed and unbrotherly conduct on the part of the rich. He thought wealth spiritually dangerous. But on the question of private property he left us no saying. In fact, Jesus' attitude toward economic matters is almost impossible for a Western man to grasp. He bade the rich young ruler sell all that he had and give the money to the poor. Apparently his own work was financed by wealthier friends. His disciples were advised to give to everyone who asked and to lend to every would-be borrower. There is no need to try to weaken his sayings. By no juggling interpretation can he be made to assume that interest in economic matters which is common both to the "businessman" and to the social reformer. Neither of these can ever be taught to pray for their daily bread and depend for it upon the God who looks after the uneconomic birds and flowers. Perhaps he intended for his disciples to work for their bread, but he does not say so.

34

His attitude toward the State was similar. Jesus seems to have obeyed the law himself, but he taught his disciples that the Sabbath was made for man, not man for the Sabbath. There is reason in Cadoux's argument that Jesus implicitly justified disobedience to the State when he reminded his followers not to fear those who could destroy only the body. Certainly the saying of the disciples, "We must obey God rather than men," would seem to be in line with their Master's teaching.

But this is really only the attitude that many ethical and religious teachers have taken. Man is to obey the law except when conscience forbids. With such teaching the Church has never been satisfied. The sayings of Jesus have been searched for centuries to find some doctrine of the State. The only one seeming to bear on the question, unless one accepts Cadoux's view that Jesus rejected judicial authority, is the famous answer to those who tried to trap him: "Render therefore unto Caesar the things that are Caesar's; and unto God the things that are God's." (Matt. 22:21.) And this says little in specific definition of the Christian's civic duties. Cadoux thinks that Jesus would have approved and co-operated in those "useful and benevolent functions that do not involve the office-bearer in any breach of the law of love." But this question, Cadoux confesses, does not actually arise in the Gospels. To illustrate the type of conclusions which are drawn from scanty sources, one may quote a more recent comment. "Evidently he felt that it was quite proper to pay taxes to Rome, since Rome minted coins, built roads, and kept order. Whether he would approve of all the taxes which Rome levied or all the extortions of the publicans is, of course, another question." [18]

The simple truth is that Jesus did not discuss those questions which so much perplex his followers today. On any assumption except that of an utterly unhistorical person uttering oracles for centuries ahead, it would be absurd to expect Jesus to pronounce upon such questions. To picture him addressing Galilean peasants on the evils of international war, on the duties of citizens in a democratic state, or on the reform of the judiciary, is only a *reductio ad absurdum* of the type of interpretation all too often used in trying to find modern ideas in his words.

Jesus preached a Kingdom of God when his will should be done on earth as it is in heaven. This conception is part of the religious inheritance of the Jewish people and as such formed the framework of his teaching. This Kingdom was made up of the meek and lowly of heart who would inherit what they could not receive in the world as they knew it. But there is no program by which the meek may assume control of the earth. There is no strategy of humility, no policy of nonresistance which is to give lordship to the good.

But Jesus not only inherited a conception of a Kingdom which he spiritualized and adapted for his own purposes. He was also a son of a people that had long struggled with the problem of organized society. Their solution had combined political and religious elements. Of the Law which the good Jew kept and which the Jewish authorities enforced, Jesus said that he came to fulfill it, not to destroy it. In the Early Church, as we shall see, the Old Testament still retained its influence. There have been many studies of the relation of Jesus to the Old Testament, but little can be determined. It is allowable to say, however, that Jesus was aware of the history of his people, of the fact that they had lived in organized community, with judicial system and with armies. If he had purposely dealt with social problems in the modern sense of that word he would undoubtedly have discussed the history of his own race.

Jesus lived in a day when his people had little part in government and had turned themselves the more to the study of their religion. He spoke to them of situations in their daily life, speaking in absolute terms. There is no need to water down his sayings, trying to prove that needles' eyes are easy passages for camels. But he spoke with oriental freedom; and no one is justified in interpreting certain sayings in a fashion which would not apply to his sayings in general. His Sermon on the Mount, despite its apparent simplicity, is subject to the same laws of interpretation as his more involved discourse.

The reader of the Gospels, therefore, should be warned that certain facts must be kept in mind. In the first place, Jesus' ethical teaching cannot be separated from his religion. There is in the Gospels no ethical system, no moral code. The assumption that there can be found in the teachings of Jesus an ethical program which can be adopted by men and nations irrespective of the religious implications of his teachings is utterly without warrant. The Christian attitude is completely and inexorably religious. "But if God doth so clothe the grass of the field, which today is, and tomorrow is cast into the oven, shall he not much more clothe you, O ye of little faith? . . . . But seek ye first his kingdom, and his righteousness; and all these things shall be added unto you." (Matt. 6:30-33.)

In the second place, the doctrine of love must not be perverted into sentimentality. As Moffatt warns us, in the teachings of Jesus "the royal Father in heaven is no easy-going deity, but One whose demands are for whole-hearted service, with stern penalties not only for those who refuse the demands, but for those who accept them and fail to obey them." [19] Talk about the Christian doctrine of love forbidding justice cannot be supported by the idea that love forgives all. There is a rejection of the Holy Spirit which is not forgiven. This is not to say that the teachings of Jesus about forgiveness do not go beyond what is called justice, or that he does not command his followers to exceed human justice; but it is to say that according to the teaching of Jesus God will punish the guilty. In the parable of the unmerciful servant whose master handed him over to torture until he had paid all that he owed, Jesus added: "So shall also my heavenly Father do unto you, if ye forgive not every one his brother from your hearts." (Matt. 18:35.)

It would seem, then, that the most careful exam-

38

ination of the passages relied upon to prove that
Jesus proclaimed a doctrine of pacifism in the sense
now attributed to that word compels the conclusion
that Jesus left no pronouncement on the question.
An attempt to prove that Jesus authorized the participation of his followers in war would reach the
same conclusion. Those who believe that Jesus expected a speedy end to the Age argue that he for this
reason disregarded the problems of society and the
State. But it is not necessary to subscribe to this view
to see that Jesus addressed himself to his hearers in
terms of the simple, everyday problems of their religion and life. And he left to other minds and to
other days the interpretation of these teachings for a
world that would sometime seem very old and the
End far off. Nor did he try to answer the questions
that his followers would have to confront when subjects had become citizens and could not escape responsibility for the society in which they lived. The
Early Church recognized this, and a tradition was
preserved that Jesus had said in his last days: "I have
yet many things to say unto you, but ye cannot bear
them now. Howbeit when he, the Spirit of truth, is
come, he shall guide you into all the truth . . . . and
he shall declare unto you the things that are to come."
(John 16:12-13.)

But for the Early Church, aliens in a land that
knew them not, cut off from a pagan society, subject
to ostracism and persecution, the message of Jesus
was clear:

Love not the world, neither the things that are in the world. If any man love the world, the love of the Father is not in him. For all that is in the world, the lust of the flesh and the lust of the eyes and the vainglory of life, is not of the Father, but is of the world. And the world passeth away, and the lust thereof: but he that doeth the will of God abideth for ever. (I John 2:15-17.)

Chapter II

FROM ST. PAUL TO CONSTANTINE

THE ATTITUDE OF THE EARLY CHURCH TOWARD
armed conflict has been studied by competent scholars, and no new references are likely to be added to
those already known. Yet any attempt to understand
the teachings of the Early Church must involve an
acquaintance with the recorded convictions of Christian writers from Paul to the Age of Constantine,
with the records left to us of the conduct of Christians during this period, and with the larger problem
of the relation of the Christian to the world.

It would seem unnecessary to remind students of
the conditions under which the early Christians lived.
But in discussions of the Early Church and war one
occasionally finds a phrase or a word which indicates
that the writer is assuming habits of mind or conditions native to later centuries but foreign to the ones
under consideration. A single example will illustrate.
A recent writer comments on Romans 13:1-8: "The
Christian is not to be a Zealot, a revolutionist, but
quietly and by spiritual means—the ballot rather than
the bullet—to achieve the desired transformation in
government." It is unnecessary to take the writer
literally: he obviously knows that the early Christians did not have ballots. But the phrase, "transformation in government," betrays the thought be-

hind it. Where in Paul is there any suggestion that the Christians are "to achieve the desired transformation in government"? This is simply to go outside the circle of ideas of the Early Church, in so far as those ideas have come down to us in writing—and that is all we have to go by.

In the first place, there was, in the earliest period, a widespread expectation of a speedy end of this world. In one of his earliest letters, even Paul seemed to expect that his generation would live to see this consummation. "For this we say unto you by the word of the Lord," he wrote to the Thessalonians, "that we that are alive, that are left unto the coming of the Lord, shall in nowise precede them that are fallen asleep." (I Thess. 4:15.) Such expectations inevitably affected the attitudes of Christians. It seems to me that Cadoux is correct when he says: "The early Christians entertained no hope that human society as a whole would be redeemed as a result of the indefinite continuation of the gradual growth of the Church. . . . . They unanimously regarded the period of Jesus' earthly life as inaugurating a final, culminating, and comparatively short epoch in human history."[1]

In the next place, it must be kept in mind that "government" to the early Christians meant either the Jewish state, so long as it existed, or the Roman Empire; and both were regarded by the Christians with a suspicion and a distaste which sometimes bordered on downright hatred. The causes for this attitude are not far to seek. The Jews, as the history of

42

Paul himself proves, often stirred up opposition to the Christians. As for the Empire, the story of the persecutions is well known. There is, indeed, a dispute as to whether there was any widespread persecution by Roman authorities until the middle of the second century. Tacitus has a story that Nero tried to shift the blame for the burning of Rome to the Christians, but there is grave doubt concerning the accuracy of the account.[2] But there was certainly a persecution in Rome as early as Nero. There may not have been empire-wide persecution of the Christians at this early date, and it was probably not a crime to be a Christian until a century later; but there is no question that there were persecutions and martyrdoms during the first century of the Church's existence. No early Christian could have seen any way to "transform" such governments as those with which he had to contend.

Other causes for a thorough distrust and dislike of contemporary government were in plenty. The cult of the Roman Emperors, with its ceremonial required by civil and military officials, offended the Christian at every turn. The most sacred words of the Christian—God, Lord, Saviour—were polluted in his eyes by their application to an earthly ruler.[3] On their part, the Romans looked with suspicion upon those who set up another Lord than Caesar, and refused to sacrifice to the Emperor. Religion was so much a part of the State in the ancient world that pagans who would otherwise not have disturbed their Christian neighbors could not explain their refusal to sacrifice except on the ground of deliberate treason. The mutual distrust of Christian and Roman citizen was aggravated by persecution, as is evident from the warnings in Paul's epistles and in First Peter. And the Book of Revelation is expressive of the bitterness against Rome which existed among Christians in the later Roman Empire. Rome was Babylon, the Mother of Harlots, and her expected downfall was hailed with rejoicing by the saints.[4]

It is well to repeat, therefore, that there was no part that an early Christian could take in government, unless he were an official, other than to obey or to disobey. And at first there was little likelihood that there would be Christian officials. Indeed, there is no concern over this possibility until the third century. (Whether there were high-placed Christians at the court of Domitian is not in point, since this was not a question of officials.) There was only one alternative for a recalcitrant subject in the Roman Empire—rebellion. And for the rebel there was little chance during the first three centuries of our era. Commentators have noticed that Paul, in warning his readers of the only end of those who disobey the powers that be, did not even think of a successful rebellion. The early Christians would have had especially little hope for a successful revolt against the Empire, since they were mainly from the lower and middle classes.[5] Their choice, therefore, was not between conforming to the State or transforming it: their choice was between obedience and disobedience.

During the early years, there was also little possibility that the Christian would be pressed as a soldier. The Jews were exempt; and at the first the Christian was regarded as a Jew. Later, the Christian was in little danger of conscription for the simple reason that the imperial levies were usually filled without the necessity of impressing men. It was as a subject in the ordinary walk of life that the Christian faced the State in those early years. He was liable to sporadic persecution and was frequently the object of local hatreds because of his alienation from many aspects of the common life. Perforce he lived as a stranger and a sojourner.

It is against this background of social conditions that the Apostle Paul's injunctions must be understood. His letters are important for the understanding of the Early Church because they were early read along with the accounts of the life and works of Jesus, and because with Paul began that wide expansion of Christianity which has gone on unto this day. It is frequently assumed that the ideas of Paul concerning government were determined by the fact that he was a Roman citizen; but they were possibly more influenced by the fact that he was a missionary. As Paul moved out through the Empire, into Asia Minor, Greece, Rome, he inevitably had to face the problem of the Christian's relation to the government.[6] And in his own statements he undoubtedly believed that he was reflecting the mind of Christ, rendering to Caesar the things that were Caesar's.

Paul's chief teaching concerning the State is Romans 13:1-7.

Let every soul be in subjection to the higher powers: for there is no power but of God; and the powers that be are ordained of God. Therefore he that resisteth the power, withstandeth the ordinance of God: and they that withstand shall receive to themselves judgment. For rulers are not a terror to the good work, but to the evil. And wouldest thou have no fear of that power? do that which is good, and thou shalt have praise from the same: for he is a minister of God to thee for good. But if thou do that which is evil, be afraid; for he beareth not the sword in vain: for he is a minister of God, an avenger for wrath to him that doeth evil. Wherefore ye must needs be in subjection, not only because of the wrath, but also for conscience' sake. For this cause ye pay tribute also; for they are ministers of God's service, attending continually upon this very thing. Render to all their dues: tribute to whom tribute is due; custom to whom custom; fear to whom fear; honor to whom honor.

The immediate occasion of Paul's words was doubtless the tendency upon the part of some Christians to adopt a hostile attitude toward the Roman Empire. Some Jewish Christians doubtless carried over such an attitude toward the Empire, but opposition and persecution would create it if it were not already there.[7] The Christian's duty, according to Paul, was to obey the powers that were: they were ordained of God to punish evil, and as such were not a terror to good men. In addition, the Empire was an actual benefit to the Church, for it stood in the way of the final evil which would come with the appearance of the Man of Sin. (II Thess. 2:1-12.) Those who feared an early End of the Age, with the accompanying tribulations for the Church, were reassured that this End would not come so long as the Empire held the evil-to-be in check.[8]

46

It is not sufficient, however, to assume that Paul's statement is simply an answer to an immediate situation in the Church. There is reason to believe that he spoke deliberately, expressing a conviction concerning the nature of the civil power. Already in Jewish Scriptures, including the rabbinical writings, political authority was said to be of God.[9] Was Paul unaware also that his view was "essentially the same theory as that of the Stoics, that man is by nature a social creature, that government is an institution necessary to the proper development of human life"?[10] The question is the more pertinent since another group in the Empire, the Epicureans, taught indifference to the State. In dealing with so catholic a mind as Paul's, one must not overlook the possibility that his statements, while not philosophical in character, were made in full knowledge of their import and of their relation to contemporary thought. Certainly, Paul's statement is explicit enough. The State demanded of the citizen, and of the subject, "custom," "fear," "honor." But the State also demanded taxes. And these taxes, "tribute," were used to maintain the order which Paul praised. It was a part of the Christian's duty to pay these taxes, not simply because they were demanded, but because they were used to preserve order. "For this cause ye pay tribute also; for they are ministers of God's service, attending continually upon this very thing."

The Christian, however, belonged also to another order. He was not to avail himself of the secular courts to settle his difficulties with his brethren. (I

Cor. 6:1-8.) He should act without regarding the world. And there was good reason for this. "But this I say, brethren, the time is shortened, that henceforth both those that have wives may be as though they had none; and those that weep, as though they wept not; and those that rejoice, as though they rejoiced not; and those that buy, as though they possessed not; and those that use the world, as not using it to the full: for the fashion of this world passeth away." (I Cor. 7:29-31.)

As to the Christian's personal life, there can be no doubt that Paul's teachings concerning humility, patience, love, are those of Jesus.

Let love be without hypocrisy. . . . Be tenderly affectioned one to another; in honor preferring one another. . . . Bless them that persecute you; bless, and curse not. . . . . Render to no man evil for evil. . . . If it be possible, as much as in you lieth, be at peace with all men. Avenge not yourselves, beloved, but give place unto the wrath of God: for it is written, Vengeance belongeth unto me; I will recompense, saith the Lord. But if thine enemy hunger, feed him; if he thirst, give him to drink: for in so doing thou shalt heap coals of fire upon his head. Be not overcome of evil, but overcome evil with good. (Rom. 12:9-21.)

This last sentence Dodd has well called "the most creative element in Christian ethics." [11]

That the principle, to overcome evil with good, is creative in Christian ethics is nowhere better shown than in the recognition that this offers a positive method of dealing with evil. That it is part of the Christian task to apply this to the changing of the world is gladly acknowledged by modern Christians. But one must not read into Paul what is not there. He did not contemplate the substitution of a Christian "strategy" for the lower but necessary task assigned by God to the powers that be, that of bringing evil men to book and of staving off the forces of darkness which would culminate in the coming of the Man of Sin.

In other books of the New Testament, there is little added to the teaching of Paul. The question of war, as war, did not arise in the sense in which it presented itself to later Christians. The wars of the Old Testament were removed from the field of controversy because they were recorded in the Old Testament. The author of the Epistle to the Hebrews unhesitatingly attributed to faith the feats of those worthies who "waxed mighty in war, turned to flight armies of aliens." (Heb. 11:34.) But the lines between the Church and the world grew more distinct as the Christians experienced the weight of the secular arm. The Christian was to live, as Paul himself had said, remembering that "the world passeth away." "If any man love the world, the love of the Father is not in him." (I John 2:15.) In the bitter experiences that must have come to many in those early days, it was hard to remember Paul's words about the divine ordination of the powers that be. For the sufferers the Apocalypse, with its burning words about the final triumph of Christ over the Beast and the pictures of blood and fire, must have seemed more nearly to express what was in their hearts.

When one turns from the books of the New Testament to the writings of Christians in the second century, the picture is not essentially changed. Most of the elements found in the canonical books appear again in the Apostolic Fathers or in the Apologists. In the Epistles of Ignatius (A.D. 90-112) is found a hatred of the "world" comparable to the attitude of the Apocalypse.[12] When the Christian is hated by the world, he is beloved of God. So deeply does Ignatius feel this that he will have nothing of any attempt to mitigate his own sufferings. The Christians of Rome are to make no attempt to free him. He is conducted by ten soldiers—ten leopards, he calls them—and if they do not kill him quickly he will persuade them to make an end of him. Only his own death can satisfy Ignatius in this struggle with the Roman power.[13] Passages from others of the early writers declaring that the Christians are law-abiding, inoffensive subjects of the Empire are too well-known to need quotation.

Nothing so far has been said about discussions of war. There seems to be a rather widespread notion that the Early Church was outspokenly pacifist during the first two centuries of its existence, perhaps even until the time of Constantine. Writers speak of the pacifism of the Early Church without explaining what they mean by the term; but it is assumed that they mean a refusal on the part of the Christian to take part in war. Even in so sober a work as the *Encyclopaedia of the Social Sciences,* one reads that the pacifist doctrine of nonresistance, including not only renunciation of war but of coercion by civil authorities, "seems to have prevailed as the normal Christian attitude for about two centuries; with the accession of Constantine to power the antimilitarist attitude of the church was abandoned." If dates mean anything, the Church is supposed to have been pacifist from the death of Paul, perhaps A.D. 65 or 70, until Constantine, who was "converted" in 312. How much justification there is for such a notion needs to be set forth.

The truth is, first, that there is no direct mention of the problem of the Christian soldier until after the middle of the second century. There are two passages in Justin Martyr (*c.*100-*c.*165), which might have been written earlier than this, that are sometimes quoted as expressing a pacifist position. In his *First Apology,* Justin declared that the prophecy of Isaiah, that the people shall beat their swords into plowshares, had been fulfilled.

For from Jerusalem there went out into the world, men, twelve in number, and these illiterate, of no ability in speaking: but by the power of God they proclaimed to every race of men that they were sent by Christ to teach to all the word of God; and we who formerly used to murder one another do not only now refrain from making war upon our enemies, but also, that we may not lie nor deceive our examiners, willingly die confessing Christ.[14]

In the *Dialogue with Trypho,* Justin repeats this.

. . . . and we who were filled with war, and mutual slaughter, and every wickedness, have each through the whole earth changed our warlike weapons,—our swords into ploughshares, and our spears into implements of tillage,—and we cultivate piety, righteousness, philanthropy, faith, and hope. . . . . sitting each under his vine, i.e., each man possessing his own married wife.[15]

These are noble words, but they must be taken for what they are. The Christians had not ceased to make war, for as a people they had never made war. They had not ended war among their neighbors. But they were a peaceful and peace-loving people. As subjects they paid taxes which supported the military and civil establishment. As for the question whether the Christian could serve in the legions, Justin says nothing about it. Until after his death, about A.D. 165, the question did not arise.

The historian Harnack, who has done most work in this field, thinks that the silence of the Christian writers during the early period is itself significant. The Christian writings deal with all manner of other problems: obedience to the State, marriage, slavery, relations with the unbeliever; but the "soldier-question" does not occur. As has been said, it was unlikely that any Christian would be a soldier during those first years. Considering the Church's emphasis upon peace and purity, it would not be expected that the Christian would seek the life of a soldier. And there was little prospect that he would be drafted. But if he were a soldier when he became a Christian, there would be the teaching of Paul: "Let each man abide in that calling wherein he was called." (I Cor. 7:20.) There were dangers for the

Christian in every calling, and those to be met by the
soldier were perhaps little greater than those endured
by the slave or the Christian married to an unbeliever.
Besides, if the End of the Age were near, there would
be little point in seeking earthly safeguards. To sum
up: the Christian was not confronted with any problem about the army, because he would hardly enter it
voluntarily; he would not likely be drafted; he would
not usually leave the army if he were converted as a
soldier. This, it need not be said, is far from a "normal" pacifist position. The "soldier-question," like
others relating to the Christian's attitude toward the
State and the social order, did not become pressing
until it was evident that the Christian would have
to deal with the State and the social order for a long
time and be answerable for his dealings.[16]

If there were soldiers in the imperial armies before
the middle of the second century, there was no occasion for mentioning them in the Christian writings.
But after A.D. 170 there are numerous references to
Christian soldiers. In a letter long attached to Justin's *Apology* is the story of the legion called the
Legio fulminata, whose Christian members prayed
for the army and were answered by rain, lightning,
and hail. The rain fell upon the parched Roman
soldiers while the lightning and hail fell upon the
enemy.[17] This letter is no longer believed to have
been written by Marcus Aurelius, but it was so accepted in the Early Church. Mention of the letter
and acceptance of it by Christian writers is evidence
that the idea of Christians in the legions was not

strange. Toward the close of the second century, Tertullian (A.D. c.160-c.230), who later became a Montanist and antimilitary in the extreme, boasted of the spread of Christianity:

. . . . we sojourn with you in the world, abjuring neither forum, nor shambles, nor bath, nor booth, nor workshop, nor inn, nor weekly market, nor any other places of commerce. We sail with you, and fight with you [*militamus*], and till the ground with you; and in like manner we unite with you in your traffickings—even in the various arts we make public property of our works for your benefit.[18]

There were Christians in the armies at least in the second half of the second century, and there is simply no evidence as to whether Christians before that time were or were not soldiers. This simple fact, in itself, fits ill with the theory that the "normal" doctrine of Christians was pacifist until the year A.D. 312. Even more important is the nature of the references to these soldiers. There is no indication that the status of soldier was regarded as *ipso facto* impossible for a Christian.

As time went on and the number of the Christians increased, the references to Christian soldiers increased also. Among these references are those to the martyrdom of soldiers. In order to understand the reasons for these martyrdoms and therefore the dangers which the Christian faced as a soldier, it will be well to look at some accounts. A famous case is recorded by Tertullian in his treatise, *Concerning the Crown*. While there was a dispensing of a special bounty to the soldiers, it seems that the privates, as well as officers, perhaps for some act of worship in connection with the imperial cult, were crowned with laurel in honor of the occasion and paraded. One soldier refused to wear the crown. To the tribune who questioned him, he replied, "I am a Christian." The case was sent to the prefects, and the accused took off his military coat, his heavy shoes, and his sword, thus renouncing his military status. Tertullian adds that "he awaits in prison the largess of Christ." [19]

Tertullian told the story as a preface to his denunciation of military service and of conforming to any pagan practice, such as wearing laurel leaves. But it is to be noted that the soldier himself objected to wearing the crown, not to being a soldier. And Tertullian says that there were criticisms of the soldier, on the ground that he was bringing trouble on his fellow Christians by disputing about "a mere matter of dress." [20] Whether these criticisms were by Christians or pagans, Tertullian did not say. Harnack seems to have been right when he said that Tertullian could cite no precedents for his belief that Christians could not be soldiers, and that his was apparently a new and unheard-of doctrine.[21]

In 298 a centurion by the name of Marcellus was executed in Africa. On the birthday of the Emperor it was required that Marcellus attend a banquet where sacrifices would be offered to the ruler. Marcellus took off his belt and his officer's insignia and announced that as a Christian he could not remain in the army. "If it is the condition of military service to sacrifice to gods and emperors," he said, "then, behold, I throw down the centurion's staff and the swordbelt, renounce my insignia and refuse to serve." Again the reason for the soldier's refusal to serve is a requirement to take part in a pagan ceremony. It has been remarked that Marcellus had advanced to the rank of centurion without having found occasion of such offense as would drive him from the army.[22]

Another instance of a Christian martyrdom will illustrate the attitude of Christians toward military service. This time it is a case of a Christian who refused to become a soldier. In 295, at Carthage, a young man, Maximilianus, who was liable to service because his father was a veteran, refused to serve and was executed. The proconsul perhaps went beyond the law in ordering the young man to death for refusal to serve. Death was legal penalty for desertion. Here is unmistakable evidence that some Christians would die rather than be soldiers. But it should be noticed that the young man's father was a veteran, and he had made a new uniform for his Christian son to wear in the army. Moreover, the proconsul seems to have been sincerely puzzled by a claim which his experience and knowledge of Christians and soldiers did not support. He reminded Maximilianus that there were Christians in the guards of the emperors; "and," he added, "they fight." [23]

In considering the Early Church's attitude toward war, other indications must be noticed. There was, as everyone knows, a widespread use of military terminology. This ought not to be pressed too far, as the use of military terms is not decisive as to what the writer thought about the possibility of a Christian's being a soldier; but it must not be ignored. If the Fathers had possessed as sensitive consciences as many modern pacifists who balk at "Onward, Christian soldiers!" many, many pages of the Early Church's writings would never have appeared. And the use of military language by the Fathers is not a late deterioration of a primitive purity. Paul's metaphors are well known. (Cf. Ephesians 6:10-20.) Clement of Rome (A.D. c.40-97) wrote to the Corinthians:

> Let us then, men and brethren, with all energy act the part of soldiers, in accordance with His holy commandments. Let us consider those who serve under our generals, with what order, obedience, and submissiveness they perform the things which are commanded them. All are not prefects, nor commanders of a thousand, nor of a hundred, nor of fifty, nor the like, but each one in his own rank performs the things commanded by the king and the generals.[24]

What effect this martial language had upon Christian thinking one cannot say. Nor can one properly assess how far such language reflected the feelings of the Church. It does make evident that the Church did not share some modern scruples.

If one cannot deduce the attitude of Christians toward serving in the army from the frequent use of military metaphors by Christian writers, it is possible to get some hints as to the normal attitude of Christians from statements which show no consciousness of conflict. Clement of Alexandria (A.D. c.150-215) has a fine passage on the knowledge of God in the various walks of life. "Practice husbandry, we say, if you are a husbandman; but while you till your fields, know God. Sail the sea, you who are devoted to navigation, yet call the whilst on the heavenly Pilot. Has knowledge taken hold of you while engaged in military service? Listen to the Commander, who orders what is right." Moffatt remarks that the significance of this passage is in the fact that Clement feels no need of arguing the point.[25] There is evidence, then, of the presence of Christians in the army, at least from the time of Marcus Aurelius. And it is evident also that there was no sense of incongruity, although always a feeling of possible danger, on the part of most of those mentioning their presence.

It must be remembered, however, that the Christians abhorred war. They bore consistent testimony that their gospel was a gospel of peace. It is this apparently which has caused some to think that every Christian writer believed it impossible for a Christian to be a soldier. No consideration of the Early Church's attitude toward war can fail to recognize that, while the "soldier-question" was not so frequently discussed and was by no means always answered in the same way, there was unanimity in the condemnation of strife.

Athenagoras, a writer of the last quarter of the second century, is not infrequently quoted as having condemned specifically the Christian soldier. But he never discussed the question. He replied to a charge that Christians were murderers by saying that, on the contrary, the Christians could not endure to see a man put to death, "though justly." They did not attend gladiatorial combats, "lest we should contract guilt and pollution"; how then, he asks, can the Christians be accused of putting people to death? [26] Cyprian (A.D. *c.*200-258), writing of the wickedness of the world, pointed to

the roads blocked up by robbers, the seas beset with pirates, wars scattered all over the earth with the bloody horror of camps. The whole world is wet with mutual blood; and murder, which in the case of an individual is admitted to be a crime, is called a virtue when it is committed wholesale. Impunity is claimed for the wicked deeds, not on the plea that they are guiltless, but because the cruelty is perpetrated on a grand scale.[27]

This was repeated, almost word for word, by Augustine and by John Wesley—and, for that matter, by scores of Christians in all ages who have detested war but have not been pacifists in the modern sense. Arnobius, who wrote at the beginning of the fourth century, believed that Christianity had greatly diminished wars.

For since we, a numerous band of men as we are, have learned from His teaching and His laws that evil ought not to be requited with evil, that it is better to suffer wrong than to inflict it, that we should rather shed our own blood than stain our hands and our conscience with that of another, an ungrateful world is now for a long period enjoying a benefit from Christ. . . . .[28]

Arnobius came nearer than Athenagoras and Cyprian to stating a pacifist position, but he did not discuss the "soldier-question." What his conclusions on this would have been we do not certainly know; but they could hardly be claimed as representing the Church's opinion, since Arnobius was "a very strange Christian." He was converted at sixty and seems to have known little of Scripture and very little of what the Christians taught.

The Christian writers of the first three centuries, then, were opposed to strife and exalted the gospel of peace. But there were soldiers who were Christians from at least the middle of the second century, if one forgets Cornelius the centurion in Luke's story. (Acts 10.) Whether there were in the second century those who held that a Christian could not serve in the legions we do not know; but Celsus, the opponent of Christianity, who wrote about the end of the second century, seems to imply that there were. The first Christian writer who definitely states the doctrine is Tertullian. He had said that Christians fought alongside others in the Empire and had seemed not to condemn this; but after he became a follower of the rigoristic Montanist sect, he came out decidedly against all participation on the part of Christians in the imperial army. Montanism was the last organized expression of hatred for the Empire, and it left its trace upon the Church, not only in the writings of Tertullian, but in a general trend toward asceticism.

Tertullian did not believe that a Christian could be a soldier even in the ranks, where he would ordinarily not be required to take part in sacrifices or be

expected to execute sentences of capital punishment.
The Lord had unbelted every soldier when he dis-
armed Peter.[29]

> Do we believe it lawful for a human oath [*sacramentum*] to
> be superadded to one divine? [he asked]. . . . Shall it be held law-
> ful to make an occupation of the sword, when the Lord proclaims
> that he who uses the sword shall perish by the sword? And
> shall the son of peace take part in the battle when it does not
> become him even to sue at law? And shall he apply the chain,
> and the prison, and the torture, and the punishment, who is not
> the avenger even of his own wrongs? . . . . And shall he keep
> guard before the temples which he has renounced? [30]

As to the duty of the soldier who becomes a Christian, Tertullian is not so clear.

> Of course, if faith comes later, and finds any preoccupied
> with military service, their case is different, as in the instance of
> those whom John used to receive for baptism, and of those most
> faithful centurions, I mean the centurion whom Christ approves,
> and the centurion whom Peter instructs; yet, at the same time,
> when a man has become a believer, and faith has been sealed,
> there must be either an immediate abandonment of it, which has
> been the course with many; or all sorts of quibbling will have to
> be resorted to in order to avoid offending God, and that is not
> allowed even outside of military service; or, last of all, for God
> the fate must be endured which a citizen-faith has been no less
> ready to accept.[31]

Tertullian's words emphasize the predicament of
the Christian soldier. He was at every step dogged
by the fear that he would be required to do something contrary to the profession of his religion. That
this was not simply shedding blood in battle is obvious

61

from Tertullian's own statement, as well as from those examples of which the proconsul reminded Maximilian: there were Christian soldiers, and they fought. The soldier might be called on to sacrifice to pagan gods, to guard pagan temples, to take an oath to a pagan emperor, or even to punish his own fellow believers. Besides, soldiering was an occupation. Men were not in for the duration of a national emergency. Tacitus has a touching picture of the veterans who revolted in Germany, showing their scars and pleading that they be retired after thirty or more campaigns.[32] This, which applied to the first century, was applicable later. There were but three choices for the Christian soldier: to quit the army, to try to avoid offense to his conscience, or to be prepared to die.

But it must be emphasized that military service was not the only hazardous occupation for Christians in the eyes of Tertullian. There were many occupations he thought unfit for Christian men. One would expect makers of images to be excluded from the Church, as also those who contributed in any way to pagan worship. But for Tertullian schoolmasters were also out of the question. They had too much to do with the names and festivals of the gods. A believer might learn literature, but he could not teach it.[33] As to whether Christians might hold civil office, Tertullian spoke in heavy irony.

So let us grant that it is possible for any one to succeed in moving, in whatsoever office, under the mere name of the office, neither sacrificing nor lending his authority to sacrifices; not farming out victims; not assigning to others the care of temples; not looking after their tributes; not giving spectacles at his own or the public charge, or presiding over the giving them; making proclamation or edict for no solemnity; not even taking oaths: . . . . neither sitting in judgment on any one's life or character, for you might bear with his judging about money; neither condemning nor fore-condemning [that is, making a law under which men would be condemned]; binding no one, imprisoning or torturing no one—if it is credible that all this is possible.[34]

According to Tertullian, then, a Christian could hold neither civil nor military office. The dangers were too great: he might be involved in idolatrous practices or in the shedding of blood. In a sterner way than Clement of Alexandria meant, the Christian was to live "in the city as in a desert." [35]

It will be worth while to consider at some length also the teachings of Origen (c.185-c.254), one of the keenest minds of the Early Church. One of his writings was in answer to a critic, Celsus, who attacked the Christians, among many other things, for their failure to assume their civic and military responsibilities in the Empire; and Origen was aware both of the force of some of Celsus' criticisms and of the problems which were raised by differences between the Old and New Testament. The Christians had come

agreeably to the counsels of Jesus, to "cut down our hostile and insolent swords into ploughshares, and to convert into pruning-hooks the spears formerly employed in war." For we no longer take up "sword against nation," nor do we "learn war any more," having become children of peace, for the sake of Jesus, who is our leader. . . . .[36]

63

Origen says frankly that the Jews could not preserve their "civil economy" if they embraced the gospel.

For Christians could not slay their enemies, or condemn to be burned or stoned, as Moses commands, those who had broken the law, and were therefore condemned as deserving of these punishments. . . . . But in the case of the ancient Jews, who had a land and a form of government of their own, to take from them the right of making war upon their enemies, of fighting for their country, of putting to death or otherwise punishing adulterers, murderers, or others who were guilty of similar crimes, would be to subject them to sudden and utter destruction whenever the enemy fell upon them; for their very laws would in that case restrain them, and prevent them from resisting the enemy.[37]

Celsus had urged that the Christians should take their part of the civic burden. As Origen quoted him, the Christians should be willing "to help the king with all our might, and to labour with him in the maintenance of justice, to fight for him; and if he requires it, to fight under him, or lead an army along with him." Origen's answer is that priests at certain shrines keep their hands unstained from blood in order that they may perform their sacrifices. Likewise the Christians keep themselves unstained that,

while others are engaged in battle, these too should engage as the priests and ministers of God, keeping their hands pure, and wrestling in prayers to God on behalf of those who are fighting in a righteous cause, and for the king who reigns righteously, that whatever is opposed to those who act righteously may be destroyed! [38]

Origen recognized the necessity of a state defending itself against enemies within and without; the Jewish state could not have existed without this defense. But the Jewish state was gone. The Christians were a nation within a nation. Not only did they not take part in war, but they declined public office.

But we recognize in each state the existence of another national organization [the phrase is hard to translate], founded by the Word of God, and we exhort those who are mighty in word and of blameless life to rule over Churches. . . . . And it is not for the purpose of escaping public duties that Christians decline public offices, but that they may reserve themselves for a diviner and more necessary service in the Church of God—for the salvation of men.[39]

This is as near to a philosophical conception of the place of the Christian society within the nation as the Fathers came to before Constantine. They maintained the Church within the nation. Therefore, they reserved their efforts to carry on the work of the Church and left to the outsiders the task of maintaining the Empire—except that the Christians prayed for the Empire, even in war, provided the war was just. And here Origen introduces the conception that was to play such a part in later Christian political thought. He recognized the necessity of force in preserving the nation, but he reserved to the Christian the right to judge whether the policy of the government were just. What position Origen would have taken in regard to the participation of the Christian in the affairs of government if he had lived to see the

65

did were moved by many considerations besides the shedding of blood in battle. Nor was there during those three centuries any situation comparable to that which a modern citizen faces when his country is invaded. The Empire was pagan; the soldier was forced often to take part in what he regarded as pagan ceremonies; his surroundings were dangerous for any man who followed purity.

From the earliest times, however, there was a tendency among some to withdraw from the "world." It is significant that those who forbade the Christian to be a soldier also forbade him to accept civil office, and for the same reasons. There was a trend away from all contacts with the life of the world toward a development of religious life in a separate community, which left the world to pursue its own way and to look after its own affairs. In Egypt by the third century there was the beginning of the great monastic movement which was to provide a refuge for all those who wished to pursue their ideal apart from the contamination of the world. But there were others—so far as we can tell, perhaps the majority—who believed that the Christian must live, as Tertullian had boasted before he became a Montanist, in the forum, in the market place, and in the camp. And these two groups we shall find all along the path of the Church's history.

Chapter III

THE CHURCH AFTER CONSTANTINE

MODERN WRITERS HAVE SOMETIMES SPECULATED whether the conversion of Constantine at the beginning of the fourth century was not one of the major catastrophes of the Church. Emerging from the catacombs, so the argument runs, the Church was weakened by an influx of worldly members, was demoralized by secular interests and corrupted by power. When the Church ceased to be a persecuted, illegal minority, it no longer struggled to maintain the original purity of the gospel, but succumbed to the secular ideals of the government. This view would not have commended itself to Christians who remembered the martyrs or who themselves had suffered. They had long prayed for relief from the dark shadow of a pagan power, and Constantine had brought deliverance from this physical terror. It is always easy to desire martyrdom when none is near, but those who have known persecution may be pardoned for welcoming peace.

The conversion of Constantine was not, so far as we can tell, the occasion of any sudden capitulation of the Church. The fourth-century Church no doubt suffered from a growing conformity to the world; but that conformity was not the inevitable result of Constantine's conversion, but of the spread of the gospel throughout the Mediterranean world. With increase of numbers came more people who shrank from the harsher demands of the gospel and were satisfied with an approximation to the faith. Naturally, when the Church was no longer outlawed some joined who would not have joined otherwise. It has been pointed out also that until long after the fourth century Christians carried over too many pagan memories to be easily conformed to the entire teachings of the Church. To this must be added the fact that the necessities of administration and organization brought subtle changes which might be deplored but apparently could not be avoided. As one historian sums it up:

> The Church had grown larger, it had developed its organization, and it was relying more on the practical men with a turn for administration, who always appear when a movement, begun by idealists, seems to show signs of success. The situation creates them, and they can not be avoided. They have their place, but they do not care for ideas.[1]

One must not, however, overestimate the effect of the growth of the Church nor of the development of its organization. It is easy, on the one hand, to idealize the first years of the Church, and, on the other, to depreciate the Christianity of later centuries. No one who remembers Simon Peter and his denial, or who has read Paul's letters to the Corinthians, will talk extravagantly about the purity of the Primitive Church; nor will those who know the fourth century with its strivings and its heartburnings speak lightly of the earnest and thoughtful men

70

of those troublous days. "We have a right to discount the common view that the church was 'paganized' or 'secularized' in this period." So speaks a competent church historian, Professor John T. McNeill. "Compromises were inevitable, but, on the whole, Christian moral idealism was not surrendered." [2]

Nevertheless, Constantine did make a difference. The Church was freed by him from the status of a prohibited society, tolerated only so long as no one chose to complain. The Emperor of the Roman Empire professed its faith and sought to promote unity within its own borders. Its bishops were honored, and its sons were promoted to office in the the State. Even the oath required of soldiers was changed, so that it no longer offended Christian consciences by exalting another Lord. In short, from a position of outlawry the Christians were suddenly invested with responsibility in the Empire. In a very real sense, the Church had to make up its mind whether it "was a sect permanently condemned to be out of touch with life as the ordinary man must live it, or whether it would attempt to be the religious guide of the world as well." [3]

And the Church made up its mind. The main line of development, as will appear in these pages, was with those who lived in the world without yielding to it, who took their part of the burden of society as one of the duties of the Christian man. This does not mean that the Church ceased to distinguish between itself and the "world." That the Empire now favored the Church in no way changed the fact that

71

the world passeth away and the fashion thereof. Only God is to be loved, and "all this world, that is, all sensible things are to be despised—while, however, they are to be used as this life requires." [4] According to Augustine, there are two kinds of blessings, temporal and eternal. "Temporal blessings are health, substance, honor, friends, a home, children, a wife, and the other things of this life in which we are sojourners. Put we up then in the hostelry of this life as travelers passing on, and not as owners intending to remain." [5] ". . . . Learn to let it [the world] go before ye are let go yourselves . . . . whilst it is with thee, loosen thy love. . . . ." [6]

Before proceeding to examine the teachings of the Church in regard to the Christian soldier, it is necessary to repeat that the Church did not suddenly reverse its attitude when it was recognized as the friend, instead of the enemy, of the Empire. The Synod of Arles, in 314 or 316, has been cited as an example of this sudden reversal of policy on the part of the Church because it forbade the admission or retention in fellowship of those who refused army service.[7] It is probable that already had begun the movement away from civil and military service on the part of those who sought refuge in the bosom of the Church from the exactions of the State. Later men sought entrance into the monasteries apparently to escape civil and military duties, and this gave no little concern to the Empire and to the Church in the time of Gregory the Great. It was necessary for the Church to guard against desertion of government on the part of those claiming to be Christians, if the members of the Church were to take their part in the life of organized society. But the best proof of the attitude of the Church is an examination of the writings of those who shaped both the thought of their own and of later times.

It is necessary to pay attention to the Church's attitude toward the State, since questions of the Christian's relation to war were inevitably bound up with larger issues. Only in moments of bitterness brought on by persecution had the Church ever thought of the State as essentially evil. It was the Apostle to the Gentiles who had said that "the powers that be are ordained of God." (Rom. 13:1.) But God had ordained the State to punish evil. Irenaeus, at the end of the second century, said explicitly: ". . . . God imposed upon mankind the fear of man . . . . in order that, being subjected to the authority of men, and kept under restraint by their laws, they might attain to some degree of justice. . . . ." [8] The State was, then, designed for moral ends. And there is a divine law which the State follows of itself because the Gentiles who "do by nature the things of the law, these, not having the law, are the law unto themselves; in that they show the work of the law written in their hearts. . . . ." (Rom. 2:14-15.)

The idea that there is a law written in men's hearts which the Gentiles may obey is close to the Stoic doctrine that right and wrong are determined by the Natural Law, which each man can discern by means of his reason.[9] It should be remarked in passing that neither Paul nor the Stoics meant that right and wrong are determined by the individual's preferences. A man discerns by his "conscience" what *is* right or wrong.[10] If men can by their rational powers determine what is the Natural Law, why is it necessary to compel them by the secular power to follow that Law? Augustine answered that, in the state of grace in which man stood before the Fall, the coercive State was not necessary. God "did not intend that his rational creature, who was made in his image, should have dominion over anything but the irrational creation. . . . .[11] By nature man is slave neither to sin nor to man.[12] But the Natural Law in its purity governed man only until sin entered the world. After sin came, the institutions of the social order became necessary; men were thereafter ruled by a relative Law of Nature. Slavery is an example, for this could never have arisen except through sin. "This servitude is . . . . penal, and is appointed by that law which enjoins the preservation of the natural order and forbids its disturbance; for if nothing had been done in violation of that law, there would have been nothing to restrain by penal servitude." [13]

But Augustine did not conceive of the social order as ordained merely for punishment of the wicked. Man is a social animal. "How much more powerfully do the laws of man's nature move him to hold fellowship and maintain peace with all men so far as in him lies. . . . ." [14] And the Heavenly City is linked with the earthly city in moral purpose. "Even the heavenly city, therefore, while in its state of pilgrim-

74

age, avails itself of the peace of earth, and, so far as
it can without injuring faith and godliness, desires
and maintains a common agreement among men regarding the acquisition of the necessaries of life, and
makes this earthly peace bear upon the peace of
heaven. . . . ." [15]   In other words, social order is not
something to which the Christian can be indifferent.
It is the fulfillment of the social nature of man, and
the destinies of the Heavenly City are in part intertwined or at least relevant to the peace of the earthly
city.

The Church after Constantine developed the doctrine which had been held since Paul, that God ordained the State as a means to promote justice in a
world which had lost its original goodness in the
Fall.   Paul did not say that every power is ordained
of God, but he spoke of a specific State which he believed to be fulfilling the divine purpose; and the
Fathers so understood him.   They believed that legitimate earthly power comes from God and is an expression of divine law. [16]   But Paul did say that Christians
should obey the divinely ordained State because it is
fulfilling a divine purpose, not merely because it is
convenient or advisable so to do.   The note of expediency had not yet entered into Christian political
philosophy.   Obedience was not for wrath, but for
conscience' sake.

In studying the positions taken by the Church after
Constantine, it is necessary to give large place to Augustine (354-430).   His was one of the greatest minds,
if not the greatest, that the Church had after Paul,

75

and he had no small advantage in that he could think politically. Such a statement certainly needs no justification in times when our own country suffers from the lack of those who can or will grasp the significance of political problems. But Augustine was first of all a Christian. Karl Burger, in *The New Schaff-Herzog Encyclopaedia,* completely misstates Augustine's point of view. He writes: "Augustine . . . . considered war a social benefit, and military service an employment of a talent agreeable to God. In his book against Faustus he exclaims, 'What is there bad in war?'" That such a statement could appear in a scholarly work is surprising, to say the least. What Augustine did was to ask the question and reply that what is bad in war is not loss of life, but moral evils let loose by war.[17] In point of fact, no one has ever written more bitingly about war than did Augustine. He quotes the pirate's words to Alexander. The king asked the pirate how he durst "molest the seas." The pirate answered: "What meanest thou by seizing the whole earth? But because I do it with a petty ship, I am called a robber: whilst thou who dost it with a great fleet art styled emperor." [18] The Roman Empire, which had brought unity to the civilized world, had bought it at a terrible price:

How many great wars, how much slaughter and bloodshed, have provided this unity! And though these are past, the end of these miseries has not yet come. For though there have never been wanting, nor are yet wanting, hostile nations beyond the empire, against whom wars have been and are waged, yet, supposing there were no such nations, the very extent of the empire itself has produced wars of a more obnoxious description—social and civil wars—and with these the whole race has been agitated, either by the actual conflict or the fear of a renewed outbreak.[19]

It was Augustine's opinion that "if any one either endures or thinks of them [i.e., wars] without mental pain, his is a more miserable plight still, for he thinks himself happy because he has lost all human feeling." [20]

It may be said here that, at least until the end of the Middle Ages, the Church did not forget the principle: *Ecclesia abhorret a sanguine*. There is blood on the history of the Church, but to the great thinkers and in the great moments of the Church this abhorrence of blood was very real. A magistrate asked Ambrose whether after pronouncing a death sentence he might come to the Lord's Supper. Ambrose replied that, inasmuch as the magistrate was acting as an executor of the laws and was therefore personally guiltless of the blood of the condemned, he would be received. But he added that if the magistrate did not come, he would be congratulated on his discrimination.[21] In 1076 a Council was held at Winchester, and the cases of certain men who had fought at Hastings with William the Conqueror were considered. These men were troubled because of the slaughter in which they engaged and because of the evils which followed. The Council decided that penances should be assessed according to the number of men which each penitent had killed. A distinction was made in the case of those soldiers who had struck down an enemy but did not know whether he had died. The

77

archers, who obviously could not know the effect of their arrows, were required to do penance one day a week for the rest of their lives.[22]   In other words, in spite of crusades and aberrations of individuals, the Church remained essentially true to her abhorrence of the shedding of blood.

Nevertheless, the Church could not escape the dilemma: should the Christian flee the world and preserve his personal purity by leaving order and government in the hands of non-Christian men; or should he imperil his peace of mind and the spotlessness of his soul by accepting his share of the burdens of society?   As in so many other matters, Augustine laid the foundation on which was built not only the Catholic doctrine of the Christian citizen, but that of the Reformers as well.

Augustine recognized that the problem of the Christian in the State was posed not only by the soldier, but by the judge.   The latter faced the possibility of condemning the innocent as well as the necessity of punishing the guilty.   Besides, the accepted judicial procedure of examining witnesses by torture was a poor way to arrive at the truth and involved in itself the possibility of wronging innocent men.   It is somewhat silly to blame Augustine and the other Fathers of the Church for not denouncing torture more vigorously.   Torture was as much a part of judicial procedure as is questioning witnesses today.   It is much easier for a modern man, with his increased sensitiveness to pain, to perceive the evils of the barbaric method than it was for an ancient or medieval man, with his experience of pest and famine and daily hardness and danger of life. It is to Augustine's credit that he saw something of the wrong inherent in the system and the problem which it created for the Christian judge.

Facing the possibilities of wrong, of actual harm to innocent persons, of the whole involved, clumsy procedure of the courts, Augustine asks the crucial question: "If such darkness shrouds social life, will a wise judge take his seat on the bench or no?" And the answer is: "Beyond question he will. For human society, which he thinks it a wickedness to abandon, constrains him and compels him to this duty." Here is one of the great sentences in the history of the Church, and it states Augustine's position on the whole matter. It is a wickedness to abandon society. He did not think of Christianity as something which was to "transform society by the Spirit of Christ," as the modern phrase has it, but he did believe that Christians cannot surrender the agencies of society to the pagans. As will be seen in a later chapter, Augustine acquiesced in the monastic provision for those who would cultivate special sanctity, but his primary conviction was that a Christian man must bear the burden of society. Yet, as he expressed this conviction, he himself recoiled from implication in human miseries. The wise man, knowing what the claim of society entails, will cry, "From my necessities deliver thou me." [23]

In considering the problem of war, Augustine could not evade the question of the Old Testament.

There were accounts of wars commanded by God. The Montanists had rejected the Old Testament, and Origen had allegorized a great deal of it. Augustine could do neither. He did not have at his hand the resources of modern literary and historical scholarship; so he could only suppose that the Wars of Jehovah were as they were said to be. In doing this he did not accent the holy war, but there is no denying that he laid a predicate for the justification of some later wars as holy. It is regrettable; but if all theologians were held accountable for the application of their teachings, there are few who would be saved. Certainly in accepting the Old Testament, rather than in rejecting it as some of the heretical sects did, Augustine obeyed a sound intuition. There is too much of value in the Old Testament to sacrifice it, and Augustine's agreement with his predecessors in his treatment of the earlier revelation was important in continuing the tradition of the Early Church. The wars of the Old Testament, Augustine thought, were enjoined to show that God has under his control and at his disposal even earthly blessings, such as temporal kingdoms and victory over enemies are considered to be. And Augustine, like Origen, had an inkling of the idea of development from Old Testament to New. In the Old, he says,

the secret of the kingdom of heaven, which was to be disclosed in due time, was veiled, and so far obscured, in the disguise of earthly promises. But when the fullness of time came for the revelation of the New Testament, which was hidden under the types of the Old, clear testimony was to be borne to the truth,

that there is another life for which this life ought to be disregarded, and another kingdom for which the opposition of all earthly kingdoms should be patiently borne.[24]

It is worth while quoting at some length from Augustine, not only to show his convictions and the arguments by which he sustained them, but to make clear that most of the questions which war raises for Christians were asked in the early centuries of the Church.

Augustine considers the assertion that the commands, "Render to no man evil for evil," and "Whosover smiteth thee on thy right cheek, turn to him the other also," are contrary to the duties of citizens. He answers that Christian teaching, if listened to, "would establish, consecrate, strengthen, and enlarge the commonwealth in a way beyond all that Romulus, Numa, Brutus, and all the other men of renown in Roman history achieved." For a State is nothing but a "multitude of men bound together by some bond of concord." And concord is what is needed in a State. "But who, even though he be a stranger to our religion, is so deaf as not to know how many precepts enjoining concord, not invented by the discussions of men, but written with the authority of God, are continually read in the churches of Christ?" And Augustine enlarges on the meaning of the "good for evil" commandments.

For these things are done only that a wicked man may be overcome by kindness, or rather that the evil which is in the wicked man may be overcome by good, and that the man may be delivered from the evil. . . . . For then it is rightly done when it seems that it will benefit him for whose sake it is done, by producing in him amendment of his ways and concord with others. At all events, it is to be done with this intention, even though the result may be different from what was expected, and the man, with a view to whose correction and conciliation this healing and salutary medicine, so to speak, was employed, refuses to be corrected and reconciled.[25]

In accordance then with this principle of concord, which is so important for the State, the Christian is to be prepared to suffer injury from those whom he desires to make good "so that the number of good men may be increased, instead of himself being added, by retaliation of injury, to the number of wicked men." But the commandment or precept pertains to the inward disposition of the heart, although the outward action may be that "which seems most likely to benefit those whose good we ought to seek." In illustration of this latter, that the outward action must be according to what is best for those whom we ought to help, Augustine reminds his readers that even our Lord, when smitten on the face, answered: "If I have spoken evil, bear witness of the evil: but if well, why smitest thou me?" (John 18:23.) And Paul, when the high priest ordered him smitten on the mouth, replied: "God shall smite thee, thou whited wall: and sittest thou to judge me according to the law, and commandest me to be smitten contrary to the law?" (Acts 23:3.)

Some things must be done, therefore, in correcting with a benevolent severity, which are against the

82

wishes of those whose welfare we seek. The Christian Scriptures have commended this virtue in a magistrate. In the correction of a son, there is assuredly no diminution of the father's love; yet sometimes it is necessary to heal by pain. In the realm of the State, wars should be carried on only with the design of making better provision for "enjoying in peace the mutual bond of piety and justice." [26]

Augustine, it should be said, does not say that killing men may teach them better ways or convert them. He does believe, however, that wars may be necessary to maintain order between nations, as the magistrate maintains peace within the nation. And he takes a realistic view of the evils of war. Poverty resulting from war is not necessarily in itself an evil. The vices which spring out of riches should be put down under any just government.[27] What are the evils of war? "Is it the death of some who will soon die in any case, that others may live in peaceful subjection? This is mere cowardly dislike, not any religious feeling. The real evils in war are love of violence, revengeful cruelty, fierce and implacable enmity, wild resistance, and the lust of power, and such like. . . . ." [28]

Augustine's conclusion is in words which he addressed to Count Boniface, governor of the Province of Africa: "Do not think that it is impossible for any one to please God while engaged in active military service." And in this letter to Boniface, Augustine gave his mature opinion concerning war.

Think, then [he wrote], of this first of all, when you are arming for the battle, that even your bodily strength is a gift of God; for, considering this, you will not employ the gift of God against God. For when faith is pledged, it is to be kept even with the enemy against whom the war is waged, how much more with the friend for whom the battle is fought! Peace should be the object of your desire; war should be waged only as a necessity, and waged only that God may by it deliver men from the necessity and preserve them in peace.[29]

In another connection he says that the just man's only concern is this: "Is the war which is to be undertaken a just one?" Just wars, according to Augustine, are usually defined as those "which avenge injuries, when the nation or city against which warlike action is to be directed has neglected either to punish wrongs committed by its own citizens or to restore what has been unjustly taken by it." [30]

This is Augustine's major contribution to the discussion of war. He was not, indeed, the first one to state a doctrine of a just war: the Stoics had already done this. But the Stoics held a doctrine of the State which a Christian could not accept. It was on Augustine's theory of justice that the Middle Ages constructed its doctrine concerning international relations. And in considering the foundations which Augustine laid, one must remember two things. First, the Christian of Augustine's day could not look upon himself as belonging only to a nation within a nation. Origen's time was two hundred years in the past, and the Christian had to choose whether to leave the responsibilities of national policy and the burdens of citizenship to the pagans or to assume them himself. If he did assume them, he was under obligation to consider the relation of the State to other peoples, as well as the relation of citizens of the State to each other. And in the second place, the barbarians at the gates of Rome could not be dismissed with a shrug. International relations were matters of fact, not dreams of what should be. For better or worse, the Church as a whole moved out along the lines indicated by their great thinker. They sought to order the relations between nations on the same principles of justice as should prevail within the State.

There is not space nor need to follow in detail the development of Augustine's doctrine through the succeeding centuries. It will be sufficient to note the elaboration or the restatement of his doctrine by some of the great thinkers of the Church who combined deep Christian interests with political insight. Thomas Aquinas (c.1225-c.1274), one of the great synthesizing minds of the Western world, gave classic statement to the doctrine of a just war. In much the same manner as Augustine he discussed the question whether it is ever right for a Christian to engage in war. After his thorough fashion, Thomas listed the arguments for the belief that a Christian should not under any circumstances go into battle. War is a punishment for sin: "He that takes the sword shall perish by the sword." War is contrary to the divine precepts: "Resist not evil"; "Avenge not yourselves. . . . ." War is contrary to the virtue of peace. The Church prohibits tournaments, which are warlike exercises; therefore it should prohibit a Christian from taking part in war. Against these arguments are set the opinions of Augustine, with which Thomas is in agreement. And Thomas proceeds to set forth his doctrine of a just war.

. . . . in order for a war to be just, three things are necessary. First, the authority of the sovereign by whose command the war is to be waged. For it is not the business of a private individual to declare war, since he can seek for redress of his rights from the tribunal of his superior. . . . . And as the care of the common weal is committed to those who are in authority, it is their business to watch over the common weal of the city, kingdom, or province subject to them. And just as it is lawful for them to have recourse to the sword in defending that common weal against internal disturbances, when they punish evil-doers . . . . so too, it is their business to have recourse to the sword of war in defending the common weal against external enemies. . . . .

Secondly, a just cause is required, namely that those who are attacked, should be attacked because they deserve it on account of some fault. . . . .

Thirdly, it is necessary that the belligerents should have a rightful intention, so that they intend the advancement of good, or the avoidance of evil. . . . .[31]

It would seem that language could hardly be plainer, but some comment may not be amiss. Thomas takes the only possible ground unless one assumes either that it is indifferent to the Christian whether the nation lives, or that a nation may survive and carry on its divinely ordained mission without attack from external enemies. Thomas assumes, on the contrary, that there should be law and order among nations as there are law and order within a nation. To maintain

86

this some use of force is necessary both within and without the nation. But the nation alone should attempt to punish those outside the nation, for within there is legal provision for the righting of wrongs. In the Middle Ages feudal organization made his provision especially necessary. Moreover, the intention of the ruler should always be right when he makes war. This is a proper mark for cheap wit; but Thomas wrote when the commission of mortal sin was expected to entail consequences which the roughest sovereign might well fear. The saint was writing for Christians; and if his limitations seem impossible to a modern man, it may be because the modern man does not take seriously the divine order which Thomas believed would eventually vindicate the Christian and insure the punishment of the ungodly.

In the centuries following the so-called Middle Ages, Catholic thought concerning war tended to flow in the stream which had been channeled by Augustine and Thomas Aquinas. Under certain circumstances it is lawful for the Christian to carry a sword; but war should be undertaken only because of crimes which cannot otherwise be punished. Only sovereign states can undertake war and then only after every other means for legal satisfaction of just claims for injuries has been exhausted. The formulation of this doctrine of the just war by the great writers was brought sharply before the Church by the colonial wars of Spain. The assertion was made, in defense of the Spanish Empire's aggressive policies in the New World, that savages could not own land because they were pagans and because they were immoral. This brought out answers from certain great Catholic moralists, who were thereby led to reconsider the whole question of the Christian and war.

It is worth while to review the conclusions of two of these Spanish writers, for their work is better known to students of international law than to ordinary readers of church history. Francisco de Vitoria (1480-1546) was a Dominican who held what was called the "primary" chair of theology at the University of Salamanca. His two important works, so far as our interests are concerned, are those concerning the Indians and concerning war. These have both been published with English translations in the series, "The Classics of International Law," by the Carnegie Institution.[32] We are not for the moment interested in his teachings concerning the rights of the Spaniards in the New World, but it will be interesting to quote at some length from his treatise *On the Law of War*.

Vitoria's work deals with four principal questions: whether Christians can make war at all; where the authority to declare or wage war reposes; what may and ought to furnish the causes for war; and what measures may be taken against the enemy in a just war. He follows the usual scholastic method, stating the proposition, giving freely and accurately the objections raised, and answering each objection before putting forth his own conclusion. He considers the Old Testament, the teachings of Jesus, the doctrine of Augustine and Thomas Aquinas; and he refers to the opinions of his contemporary, Martin Luther. He thinks that it is clear that a defensive war can be waged. But he is also sure that an offensive war may be undertaken when one is seeking to repossess property or trying to avenge wrongs. A defensive war could not be waged satisfactorily unless the enemy were punished, for otherwise the offender would only be emboldened to make a second attack. Since the end and aim of war is the peace and security of the State, enemies must be made to desist from warlike effort. "For the situation with regard to war would be glaringly unfair, if all that a State could do when enemies attack it unjustly was to ward off the attack and if they could not follow this up by further steps."

He believed that even a private person can repel force by force. There may be occasions when he should flee and escape, but his honor and reputation may demand that he stand. There is a difference, however, between a private person and a State. For while the private person has a right to defend himself and what belongs to him, he has no right to avenge a wrong done to him,

nay, not even to recapt property that has been seized from him if time has been allowed to go by since the seizure. But defense can only be resorted to at the very moment of the danger, or, as the jurists say, *in continenti*, and so when the necessity of defense has passed there is an end to the lawfulness of war.

According to Vitoria, one may strike back when the assaulter does not propose to make a further at-

89

tack if it is necessary thus to avoid shame and disgrace.

As to the reasons and causes of just wars, Vitoria is moved to answer certain questions because of the problems raised by the Indians whose case he is considering. He believes that "difference of religion is not a cause of just war." Neither is the extension of empire a just cause, nor "the personal glory of the prince, nor any other advantage to him." His opinion is that there is only one just cause for commencing a war, "namely, a wrong received." Nor can every kind and degree of wrong suffice as a reason for war.

The proof of this is that not even upon one's own fellow-countrymen is it lawful for every offense to exact atrocious punishment, such as death or banishment or confiscation of property. As, then, the evils inflicted in war are all of a severe and atrocious character, such as slaughter and fire and devastation, it is not lawful for slight wrongs to pursue the authors of the wrongs with war, seeing that the degree of the punishment ought to correspond to the measure of the offense.

Vitoria is a realist and does not shirk the unpleasant consequences of his own theory. He believes that in war everything is lawful which "defense of the common weal requires." Expenses of the war and damages may be made good out of enemy property. The enemy's fortresses may be destroyed and even one built on enemy soil if this is necessary to avoid attack. But he is careful to say that deliberate slaughter of the innocent is never lawful any more than it is lawful within a state to punish the innocent

90

for the wrongdoer. Even in a war with the Turks it is not allowable to kill women and children. Harmless agricultural folk, and the rest of the peaceable civilian population who are presumed to be innocent, must be protected. Nevertheless, it is sometimes necessary to slay the innocent even knowingly, "as when a fortress or city is stormed in a just war, although it is known that there are a number of innocent people in it, and although cannon and other engines of war cannot be discharged or fire applied to buildings without destroying the innocent together with guilty." It is lawful to take goods that are needed in repayment of wrong done, but there must be no killing of children because of fear that they may grow up to be enemies.

It is not enough for a prince to believe that he is right.

And for proof I rely, first, on the fact that in some matters of less moment it is not enough either for a prince or for private persons to believe that they are acting justly. This is notorious, for their error may be vincible and deliberate, and the opinion of the individual is not enough to render an act good, but it must come up to the standard of a wise man's judgment. . . . .

An exceedingly careful examination must be made of the justice and causes of the war.

For truth and justice in moral matters are hard of attainment and so any careless treatment of them easily leads to error, an error which will be inexcusable, especially in a concern of great moment involving danger and calamity to many, and they our neighbors, too, whom we are bound to love as ourselves.

91

If the prince must be careful to determine the justness of his cause before undertaking war, what about the subject? "On this doubt let my first proposition be: If a subject is convinced of the injustice of a war, he ought not to serve in it, even on the command of his prince." However, under ordinary circumstances it is sufficient for "men of the lower order, even if they perceived the injustice of a war," since they cannot stop it and their voice would not be heeded, to serve in it "in reliance on their betters." It is enough for them if they wage a war that is undertaken after public counsel and by public authority. Nevertheless, there are some wars whose injustice is so evident "that ignorance would be no excuse even to subjects of this sort who serve in it."

Vitoria brings out one point that is new. There is an obligation upon the prince and his followers to see that greater evils do not arise out of a war than the war would avert.

For if little effect upon the ultimate issue of the war is to be expected from the storming of a fortress or fortified town wherein are many innocent folk, it would not be right, for the purpose of assailing a few guilty, to slay the many innocent by use of fire or engines of war or other means likely to overwhelm indifferently both innocent and guilty.

A war may be just and lawful in itself and yet unlawful owing to some collateral circumstances,

for inasmuch as wars ought to be waged for the common good, if some one city cannot be recaptured without greater evils befalling the State, such as the devastation of many cities, great slaughter of human beings, provocation of princes, occasions for new wars to the destruction of the Church (in that an opportunity is given to pagans to invade and seize the land of Christians), it is indubitable that the prince is bound rather to give up his own rights and abstain from war. For it is clear that if the King of France, for example, had a right to retake Milan, but by the war both the Kingdom of France and the Duchy of Milan would suffer intolerable ills and heavy woes, it would not be right for him to retake it. This is because that war ought to take place either for the good of France or for the good of Milan.

Vitoria's conclusions are in three canons on the ethics of war. Although a prince has authority to make war, he should, "first of all, not go seeking occasions and causes of war." He should reflect "that others are his neighbors, whom we are bound to love as ourselves," for "it is the extreme of savagery to seek for and rejoice in grounds for killing and destroying men whom God has created and for whom Christ died." When war for a just cause has broken out "it must not be waged so as to ruin the people against whom it is directed, but only so as to obtain one's rights and the defense of one's country and in order that from that war peace and security may in time result." The third canon directs that when victory has been won, it "should be utilized with moderation and Christian humility, and the victor ought to deem that he is sitting as a judge between two States, the one which has been wronged and the one which has done the wrong." And the judgment should involve the offending State "in the least degree of calamity and misfortune."

One other example should be given of Catholic

thought in the sixteenth century. Suárez (1548-1617) was a Jesuit, who was born at Grenada. His treatment of war, like that of Thomas Aquinas, is found under the larger heading of charity, in a theological work entitled *Concerning the Threefold Theological Virtue.* Like Francisco de Vitoria, Suárez combats the contention that the barbarians are incapable of self-government, and that one can follow the teaching of Aristotle that a war is naturally just when directed against those born to obey. It is evident, said Suárez, that there are many infidels who are more intelligent than some Christians and more apt in the matter of government. Suárez does, however, extend the doctrine of probabilism to the question of war, holding that the prince may act upon the more probable reason when he is not sure of his right. In this Suárez went far toward justifying wars for "reasons of state." But, on the whole, he took the traditional position that a Christian prince must not go to war unless because of a violation of right or to defend the innocent.[33]

That the Church was not always true to its own doctrine goes without saying. Nor was it able to tame the fierce spirit of the troubled centuries when the barbarians were learning to live in settled communities and to form national states. With the breakdown of the old economic order, the discovery of the New World, the rupture of the ecclesiastical unity of the Middle Ages, new forces were released which no prophet had foreseen and no institution could control. But the Church had given to the world a

94

doctrine of international order and international justice. Attempts to enforce this order had resulted in the little-effective Truce of God and in the claims of the papacy to be the arbiter of the nations. Yet the principles of justice between nations had been laid down. The ruler must enforce peace within his own borders, and, if necessary, between his nation and others. But no rule of expediency or of national aggrandizement was recognized by the great thinkers of the Church. The principles of the Church, especially those of the Spanish School, were the foundations for Grotius' great work, *On the Law of War and Peace*. And the world yet awaits an international organization which can enforce impartially the justice between nations which from the time of Augustine the Church demanded.

Chapter IV

MONKS AND SECTARIES

THE PREVIOUS CHAPTER HAS FOLLOWED THE MAIN
stream of Catholic teaching concerning the Church
and war from Augustine to the writers of the sixteenth century. Much of this stream is the common inheritance of Christians—Catholic and Reformed. But there were always those who were not
satisfied to dwell in a world of market places, of
courts and camps, and sought to live a more perfect
life under conditions in which they might be free
from those claims of society which Augustine
thought the just man could not deny. One meets
frequent references in books about peace and war to
one small group in the Middle Ages, the Waldenses;
but that the great monastic movement was also, in
part, a flight from the world is often ignored. The
groups within the Catholic Church of the Middle
Ages who thought to cultivate perfection away from
the contamination of secular society were accom-
modated in the monastic orders. Those who broke
with the Church but sought evangelical perfection
were in certain sects whose "pacifism" was only a part
of their life and doctrine. Both need to be understood by the student who would properly assess the
attitudes of Christians toward war throughout the
Christian centuries.

96

Now it was not six months after the death of his parents, and going according to custom into the Lord's House, he communed with himself and reflected as he walked how the Apostles left all and followed the Saviour; and how they in the Acts sold their possessions and brought and laid them at the Apostles' feet for distribution to the needy, and what and how great a hope was laid up for them in heaven. Pondering over these things he entered the Church, and it happened the Gospel was being read, and he heard the Lord saying to the rich man, "If thou wouldest be perfect, go and sell that thou hath and give to the poor; and come follow me and thou shalt have treasure in heaven.[1]

It is with the words, "If thou wouldest be perfect," that monasticism began. The eighteen- or twenty-year-old boy who was to be famous as St. Anthony heard these words, sold all that he had, and gave the proceeds to the poor. Thus the father of the monastic movement began his work.

Scholars have debated whether asceticism in the Church stemmed out of extraneous influence, from Buddhism, Neoplatonism, Stoicism, or from the Essenes. But it is immaterial what outside forces may have been at work. There is enough in the New Testament to account for the desire of Christians to separate themselves from the world in order to live a perfect life. "Ye therefore shall be perfect, as your heavenly Father is perfect" (Matt. 5:48), said the Great Teacher. And the Imitation of Christ always haunted the Church as an ideal. "For hereunto were ye called: because Christ also suffered for you, leaving you an example, that ye should follow his steps: who did no sin, neither was guile found in his mouth: who, when he was reviled, reviled not

again; when he suffered, threatened not; but committed himself to him that judgeth righteously. . . . ."
(I Pet. 2:21-23.)

Modern writers, especially Protestants, find it difficult to appreciate the motives which drove men into the deserts or into monasteries to practice austerities, or at least to observe the primary vows of poverty, chastity, and obedience. This difficulty is not confined to the Protestant, but is partly a result of modern ways of thinking. Even Roman Catholics today find it necessary to assert that the objects of asceticism were in part to confer social benefits.[2] But there were words in the New Testament which could be interpreted as enjoining men for their own salvation to become "athletes" of Christ.

> Know ye not that they that run in a race run all, but one receiveth the prize? Even so run; that ye may attain. And every man that striveth in the games exerciseth self-control in all things. Now they do it to receive a corruptible crown; but we an incorruptible. I therefore so run, as not uncertainly; so fight I, as not beating the air; but I buffet my body, and bring it into bondage: lest by any means, after that I have preached to others, I myself should be rejected. (I Cor. 9:24-27.)

And in words attributed to Paul the Church had directions that could be understood in a warring world. "No soldier on service entangleth himself in the affairs of this life; that he may please him who enrolled him as a soldier." (II Tim. 2:4.)

So long as the Christians were few in number and subject to ostracism, if not to persecution, by their neighbors, there was little need for members of the

Church to seek separation from the world. The world stood ready to enforce that separation and even to provide ways whereby the Christian might follow his Lord to the cross. But as the numbers of Christians increased, and especially as the power of the persecuting pagans waned, there were many in the Church who sought uneasily for means whereby they could escape the entanglements of the world.

The earnest man found in the sayings of Jesus and of Paul much that distressed his conscience. The rich young ruler had kept all the commandments from his youth up, and Jesus had said to him: "If thou wouldest be perfect, go, sell that which thou hast, and give to the poor. . . . ." (Matt 19:21.) The disciples had asked Jesus whether it is good for a man to marry, and he had answered: ". . . . there are eunuchs, that were so born from their mother's womb: and there are eunuchs, that were made eunuchs by men: and there are eunuchs, that made themselves eunuchs for the kingdom of heaven's sake. He that is able to receive it, let him receive it." (Matt. 19:12.) And Paul had spoken in terms which, while they legalized marriage, left the reader uncertain as to the desirability of it.

Now concerning virgins I have no commandment of the Lord: but I give my judgment, as one that hath obtained mercy of the Lord to be trustworthy. I think therefore that this is good by reason of the distress that is upon us, namely, that it is good for a man to be as he is. Art thou bound unto a wife? seek not to be loosed. Art thou loosed from a wife? seek not a wife. But shouldest thou marry, thou hast not sinned; and if a

99

virgin marry, she hath not sinned. Yet such shall have tribulation in the flesh; and I would spare you. . . . . But I would have you to be free from cares. He that is unmarried is careful for the things of the Lord, how he may please the Lord: but he that is married is careful for the things of the world, how he may please his wife, and is divided. (I Cor. 7:25-34.)

Was it necessary then for the Christian who sought perfection to sell all that he had and give to the poor? Was it better that he should abstain from marriage? How, in the light of these sayings from the Holy Writings, could a Christian entangle himself with the things of the world? These were, indeed, not all the Christian's problems. In the turbulent world of the first three centuries of the Church, one's life and property were preserved only by the Roman sword; and in the years when the barbarians came down like locusts, not even the Roman sword was sufficient. But there were the sayings of the Gospels:

. . . . but I say unto you, Resist not him that is evil: but whosoever smiteth thee on thy right cheek, turn to him the other also. And if any man would go to law with thee, and take away thy coat, let him have thy cloak also. And whosoever shall compel thee to go one mile, go with him two. Give to him that asketh thee, and from him that would borrow of thee turn not thou away. (Matt. 5:39-42.)

Poverty, chastity, passive obedience—all these were ideals which disturbed sensitive consciences.

It has been noted that certain Fathers of the Church counseled Christians to abstain from all civil and military service; but it is necessary now to note in more detail the admonitions to poverty and

100

chastity, as well as to nonresistance or nonparticipation of the Christian in civil duties. Tertullian, for example, who was the first to declare that the Christian should not be a soldier, was very clear in his preference of celibacy over marriage. "For the apostle," he says, "although preferring the grace of continence, yet permits the contraction of marriage and the enjoyment of it, and advises the continuance therein rather than the dissolution thereof." This much for Paul. As for Tertullian, ". . . . we do not reject marriage, but simply refrain from it." [3] Cyprian spoke of virgins as the glory of the Church. "The glorious fruitfulness of Mother Church rejoices by their means and in them abundantly flourishes. . . . ." [4] Jerome's letters on virginity are, of course, famous; but they must not be disregarded, for they not only influenced the Church, but in much were representative of contemporary opinion. In his letter to the Lady Eustochium, Jerome praised wedlock because of wedlock are born virgins. "I praise wedlock, I praise marriage, but it is because they give me virgins. . . . ." He will not hear to those who pretend that Paul was married. The Apostle had no commandment from the Lord concerning virginity because it would have been a hard enactment to compel opposition to nature "and to extort from men the angelic life." [5] Augustine himself discussed at great length the place of virginity in the scale of Christian virtues. While he guarded against any denunciation of marriage, even he made it very clear that virginity was to be preferred to marriage. And the preference

101

understood merely as a withdrawal from the world. The perfection sought by the great monks was perfection in love, and one could not write the history of monasticism without also taking account of the mystical search for oneness with God on the part of some of the saints of the monasteries. Nevertheless, renunciation of the world was a definite part of the monastic ideal.

Montalembert, the well-known historian of monasticism, has argued that the monks retired from the world, not because they were weak, but because they were strong. Indeed, the monks were, in the thinking of their contemporaries, the soldiers of Christ par excellence.[10] But Jerome did not hesitate to say that it was good strategy in the soldier of Christ to avoid the conflicts of the world. In his intemperate letter against Vigilantius, who had protested the extravagances of Jerome and his followers, he said:

Why, you will say, go to the desert? The reason is plain: that I may not hear or see you; that I may not be disturbed by your madness; that I may not be engaged in conflict with you; that the eye of the harlot may not lead me captive; that beauty may not lead me to unlawful embraces. You will reply: "This is not to fight, but to run away. Stand in line of battle, put on your armor and resist your foes, so that, having overcome, you may wear the crown." I confess my weakness. I would not fight in the hope of victory, lest some time or other I lose the victory.[11]

In the retirement into which the anchorite, and later the monk, went, "there was neither the evil-doer, nor the injured, nor the reproaches of the tax-gatherer." [12] The ordinary cares of life did not disturb the seeker after perfection. "There is no fear there, or trembling; no ruler accuses, no wife provokes, no child casts into sadness, no disorderly mirth dissipates, no multitude of flatterers puff up; but the table is an angel's table free from all such turmoil." "There are not master and slaves; all are slaves, all free men." [13]

The hermit and the monk are spoken of frequently as being dead to the world. "Is not every monk an exile from his country?" asked Jerome. "Is he not an exile from the whole world?" [14] In the thirteenth century, Jacques de Vitry told of a monk whose brother begged something and was told to go and ask another brother. The beggar said, "You know that he is dead and no longer in the world." The monk replied, "I, too, am dead." A novice, according to another story, was sent by his abbot to bless and to curse the bones of the dead. When the novice returned, he was asked what answer the bones had made. He answered that the bones made no reply at all. Then said the abbot, "Thus it behooves thee to be dead if thou wishest to remain in this monastery." [15]

The extent to which the monks were supposed to be cut off from the world may be seen from the famous Rule of St. Benedict, who in the sixth century provided the basis upon which most future monastic establishments were organized.[16] Benedict introduced into monasticism the principle of "stability," that is, the principle that monks could not change monasteries. According to the Benedictine

Rule, when visitors came to a monastery, "no one shall venture to talk to a guest or to associate with him; and when a brother meets one, he shall greet him humbly, and ask his blessing, but shall pass on, explaining that it is not permitted to the brothers to talk with guests." [17] A monk was not supposed to receive letters or gifts from his family or from others outside the monastery, nor was he to send anything except by the command of the abbot. A chapter, which may be a later addition to the Rule, provided that those who were sent on errands outside the monastery should not relate to their brethren anything that they saw or heard while in the world: "for herein lies the greatest danger of worldly contamination." [18] It must be remembered, of course, that these rules were not always kept. It has been remarked that some of the great chroniclers of the Middle Ages were monks, who must have obtained much of their information from visitors. But the ideal was complete isolation from the world.

Since the time of Martin Luther, an argument has gone on as to whether the monks believed that salvation depended upon entrance into the monastic life.[19] Professor Coulton is sure that in St. Bernard's day few men doubted "that monachism was *the* heavenly way. The common word for a monastic Order was *Religio,* and the ordinary sense of *Conversio,* even in Canon Law, was 'taking the monastic vow'; it may safely be said that medieval writers use it half a dozen times in this sense for once that they use it in Wesley's sense." [20] For the present purpose, it is not important to determine whether the ordinary man in the Middle Ages thought that the monastic life was necessary to salvation. Certainly the call to this life was presented as evangelists present the need of conversion. Jacques de Vitry has a story of a noble youth, the only son of his parents, who entered a monastery without their knowledge. The grieved and outraged father threatened to burn the abbey if his son were not returned to him. The youth asked for a horse and went to meet his father. The son explained to his father that he had left home and had taken the monastic habit because of a dangerous custom which prevailed in his father's territory. The father promised that all the customs of the land would be revoked if his son desired it. Then the son replied that the custom to which he referred was that in his father's land the young died as well as the old. The father thereupon forsook the world and entered the monastery with his son.[21]

Nowhere is the tension caused by a desire to follow literally the words of the New Testament and the claims of social life more apparent than in the history of monasticism. It is easy for the modern reader to say that our Lord was not laying down universal laws when he said to the rich young ruler: "Go, sell that which thou hast." But the modern reader must remember that just that problem presents itself to those who see in the words, "turn the other cheek," a universal rule of life applicable at all times and in all places. To the man of the Middle Ages there had to be some solution of the intolerable dilemma in

107

which he found himself. On the one hand, he knew quite well that, if every man refused to have a family, refused to own property, refused to help maintain law and order within and without the State, social life was impossible. What, then, of the incontrovertible sayings, that it were better for a man not to have a wife, that there were eunuchs for the kingdom of heaven's sake, that if one were to be perfect he should sell all that he had, that when smitten one should turn the other cheek? Modern scholarship had not come along to emphasize historical and literary interpretations; and experience has shown how little that scholarship has been able to do even in the twentieth century to insure rational understanding of the New Testament. The solution to which the medieval Church came is that which critics in later centuries were to call "double morality."

This solution was to recognize a difference between that which was commanded and that which was advised. One was necessary for salvation, the other necessary for the perfect life. In one of his letters, Jerome quotes the words of the Lord, "If thou wouldest be perfect," and adds:

Great enterprises are always left to the free choice of those who hear of them. Thus the Apostle refrains from making virginity a positive duty, because the Lord in speaking of eunuchs who had made themselves such for the kingdom of heaven's sake finally said: "He that is able to receive it, let him receive it." . . . . There is no compulsion laid upon you. If you are to win the prize it must be by the exercise of your own free will.[22]

108

As usual, Augustine stated the doctrine for the Church.

There are [he said] sins, which are restrained by command not by counsel, on this account, because it is matter of condemnation not to obey the Lord when he commands. . . . . For whosoever obeys not a command, is guilty and liable for punishment. Wherefore, because it is not sin to marry a wife or to be married, (but if it were a sin, it would be forbidden by a "command,") on this account there is no "command" of the Lord concerning virgins. But since, after we have shunned or had forgiveness of sins, we must approach eternal life, wherein is a certain or more excellent glory, to be assigned not unto all who shall live for ever, but unto certain there; in order to obtain which it is not enough to have been set free from sins, unless there be vowed unto Him, Who setteth us free, something, which it is no matter of fault not to have vowed, but matter of praise to have vowed and performed; he sayeth, "I give counsel, as having obtained mercy from God that I should be faithful." [23]

In other words, Paul's statement, that he did not have a "commandment" from the Lord concerning virgins but that he did give "counsel" on the matter, became the basis for a doctrine of the "evangelical counsels." Thomas Aquinas distinguishes between commands and counsels as between that which is essential and that which is instrumental to obtain the end desired. The counsels are given to the end that there may be removed whatever is not contrary to love but is a hindrance, such as marriage, being concerned with secular business, and the like.[24] The commands have to be obeyed; the counsels are optional. True, a man may use the things of this world and reach the goal of the Christian life, but he will more quickly attain the end desired by giving up entirely the goods of this world.[25]

The evangelical counsels were commonly understood as poverty, chastity, and obedience; but these three implied practically the whole of the Imitation of Christ. There is little reference in the sources to the "soldier-problem" as affecting the monks. The separation of the monk from the world included separation from military as well as civil responsibilities. Indeed, there are signs that in the early centuries there was some difficulty because men fled to the monasteries to escape their responsibilities. In 377, Valens promulgated a law imposing military service upon the monks of Nitria. This law was repealed two years later and seems to have been designed only against monks who had been subjects of complaints.[26] In 593, Pope Gregory the Great received an edict from Constantinople forbidding anyone engaged in public service from taking ecclesiastical office or from retiring into a monastery. The edict also forbade soldiers from becoming monks until after retirement from the army. Gregory agreed there was no point in public officials' taking ecclesiastical office, but he objected strongly to the provision concerning soldiers. "This ordinance, I confess to my lords," he wrote, "has alarmed me greatly, since by it the way of heaven is closed against many, and what has been lawful until now is made unlawful." Gregory was himself a monk who had been raised to the papal chair, and he believed heartily that for many monasticism meant salvation. He said as much to his imperial superiors. "For there are many who are able to live a religious life even in secular condition: but there are very many who can not in any wise be saved with God unless they give up all things." Gregory knew that all soldiers did not turn monk for impure reasons, for he had himself known some who had worked miracles and had "wrought signs and mighty deeds." After a few years, Gregory seems to have become reconciled to the edict. It is probable that upon investigation the pope found that men were using the monasteries as a way to escape their civil and military obligations. At any rate, Gregory advised that greater care be used lest soldiers become monks merely to avoid the hardship of military service.[27]

It is well known that the monastic vows were violated, and that successive reforms were necessary among the Orders. In the confused centuries which are really the "dark ages," that is, from the sixth to the tenth centuries, monasteries at times may have had to defend themselves against robbers or turbulent neighbors. At any rate, St. Thomas says that members of a religious Order may fight, if it is certain that they are not fighting to gain worldly ends, but to protect the Church, public order, or in defense of the poor or oppressed. And he quotes St. Ambrose: "The courage, whereby a man in battle defends his country against barbarians, or protects the weak at home, or his friends against robbers, is full of justice. . . . ."[28] It was on this principle that the military Orders, such as the Templars, were organized. Dr.

111

Workman says that the military Orders were a middle state in a slow process of the development of monasticism. Originally, monasticism held that if a man would serve God best he must quit the world. The military Orders were founded on the principle that if a man would serve God he must fight the world. With St. Francis came the principle that if a man would serve God he must serve the world.[29] Nevertheless, with the military Orders one reaches a change in the monastic ideal. Originally, the monastic movement was partly (and I recognize that it was only partly) a response to the Christian's problem of reconciling ordinary life with the literal interpretation of the commandments and counsels of the gospel. Before leaving the subject, one more illustration may be added to confirm this point.

One finds in the records evidence that some sensitive souls were not content with poverty, chastity, and obedience as fulfilling the needs for an Imitation of Christ. There was within the monastic communities difficulty with those who insisted upon a more literal following of the sayings of the New Testament. One example will suffice. Augustine wrote at some length exhorting monks to work with their hands. One of the objections that he met was based upon the words of our Lord concerning the fowls of the air: "Behold the birds of the heaven, that they sow not, neither do they reap, nor gather into barns; and your heavenly Father feedeth them. Are not ye of much more value than they?" (Matt. 6: 26.) Why, then, asked the monks, should they work

112

with their hands? Obviously, they should expect the Father to feed them. Augustine replied with heavy sarcasm: it would be well if the Lord "should deign to bestow wings also, that the servants of God being found in other men's fields should not be taken up as thieves, but as starlings to be scared off." [30] Augustine was a practical man and also a scholar. It was hard for him to sympathize with the aberrations of those who would turn the words of our Lord into laws out of a statute book. Yet Augustine himself sympathized fully enough with the aspirations of those who would leave the world to seek perfection away from the market place and the camp.

Those who seem to believe that the Church was, in its original purity, pacifist say very little about the monastic Orders; but they frequently quote St. Francis of Assisi (1182-1226). Indeed, the nineteen-twenties saw a number of books and articles on St. Francis, perhaps a symptom of the need for escape in that troubled decade. Undoubtedly, no man has ever embodied the desire to follow literally in the footsteps of Christ more than did Francis. With him the monastic ideal came out of the monastery into the streets and into the countryside. But one should know exactly what Francis believed to be the way of perfection. It is neither historically accurate nor morally justifiable to quote Francis as if he were merely a preacher of Tolstoyan simplicity of life, or as if he advocated a Christianity which could be practiced by a modern man who draws a salary, lives with his family and provides for them after the usual

113

fashion even of religious people, and takes part in the political and social affairs of his country.

It was possibly in 1209 that Francis entered the little chapel at Assisi, which he prepared with his own hands while yet uncertain of his mission. When the priest turned toward him to read the words of Jesus, Francis felt that Jesus himself was speaking.

And as ye go, preach, saying, The kingdom of heaven is at hand. Heal the sick, raise the dead, cleanse the lepers, cast out demons: freely ye received, freely give. Get you no gold, nor silver, nor brass in your purses; no wallet for your journey, neither two coats, nor shoes, nor staff: for the laborer is worthy of his food. (Matt. 10:7-10.)

Immediately, Francis threw away his purse, his shoes, and his stick.[31]

It was to this mission of preaching and serving that he called his followers. There was to be utter humility and a literal obedience to the counsels of the gospel. Once, in winter, Francis and Brother Leo were returning to the little chapel in Assisi. Francis spoke to Brother Leo of perfect joy. It was not, he said, in giving sight to the blind, in healing the sick, even in raising the dead. It was not in speaking the language of angels, not even in converting all the infidels. Very naturally Brother Leo asked what perfect joy is. To this the Saint replied:

When we arrive at Santa Maria degli Angeli, soaked with rain, frozen with cold, covered with mud, dying of hunger, and we knock and the porter comes in a rage, saying, "Who are you?" and we answer, "We are two of your brethren," and he says, "You lie, you are two lewd fellows who go up and down corrupting the world and stealing the alms of the poor. Go away from here!" and he does not open to us, but leaves us outside shivering in the snow and rain, frozen, starved, till night; then, if thus maltreated and turned away, we patiently endure all without murmuring against him, if we think with humility and charity that this porter really knows us truly and that God made him speak thus to us, then, O Brother Leo, write that in this is the perfect joy.[32]

No monastic Rule ever implied more self-abnegation nor further separation from secular interests than this story indicates. And Francis' scale of evangelical values is plain enough. For laymen and laywomen who adhered to the Order which he seems to have designed, he provided less strict regulation. Indeed, Sabatier thinks that he did not design a Third Order, but only a life of evangelical simplicity. Those not within the Order were to give away all that they could, keeping only what was strictly necessary. They were to minister to the sick and needy. Under no circumstances were they to bear arms.[33] This in itself would have prevented men and women from carrying on ordinary life as it was lived then and is lived now. But the real mission of Francis was to call his followers to his own strict ideals.

The center of this ideal was poverty. Of his devotion to poverty the stories are almost endless, and Giotto's famous painting, "The Marriage of Francis to Poverty," indicates truly the dominance of the idea in the Saint's thinking. According to the *Speculum perfectionis*, Francis once said to a brother of noble birth: "I tell thee, Brother, that this was and is my first and last intention and desire, if the brethren would have believed me, that no friar should have anything save a robe, as our Rule allows us, with a girdle and breeches." [34] A novice who could read, although not well (*licet non bene*), had received from his superior permission to own a psaltery. But the novice was not satisfied without securing Francis' permission also. The Saint replied that many desired honor and praise for reading and preaching what the saints had done, indicating that it is better to do than to read about others' actions. Again the novice approached Francis about the psaltery. Francis said: "After you have a psaltery, you will want to have a breviary. Then you will sit in your chair, like a great prelate, and say to your brother, 'Bring me the breviary!' " Several months later the brother mentioned the matter again. Francis told him to go ahead and get the psaltery as his superior had allowed. But when the novice turned away, Francis called him back and asked him to point out the exact spot where they had stood when the permission was given. Arrived at the place Francis knelt down and cried: "*Mea culpa, frater, mea culpa,*" adding, "for whosoever will be a Friar Minor should have nothing except a tunic, as the Rule concedes to him, and a cord and breeches, and those who are forced by manifest necessity, sandals." [35]

It is necessary to emphasize this passion for poverty on the part of St. Francis, because it was a major element in his separation from the world. There is, of course, the element of literalness in insistence upon taking neither two coats nor shoes. But there was a

116

deep-seated conviction in Francis that separation from the world begins with poverty. Innocent III hesitated on this account to approve the new Order. He doubted whether the successors of Francis would be able to adhere so rigidly to the vow of poverty.[36] But, as Sabatier puts it, "money was truly for him the sacrament of evil." [37] The *Speculum perfectionis* tells how a layman entered the chapel of Assisi to pray and put some money for an offering near the cross. One of the brethren picked up the money and put it in a window. But he had touched money, and the matter was reported to Francis. The offending brother threw himself upon the ground, asking for mercy. Francis commanded him to take the money in his mouth and deposit it on the dung of an ass. And the *Speculum* adds: "And all that did see and hear were filled with very great fear, and from that time forth did despise money more than the dung of an ass, and daily were they animated with new examples to condemn it altogther." [38]

There is no place here to notice the strife that broke out in the Order, especially after Francis' death, over the principle of absolute poverty. Although Sabatier may overemphasize the departure of later Franciscans from the ideals of the Founder, and although the *Speculum* itself is a document written with a purpose, there is general agreement that Francis himself enforced poverty as a major requirement. And he did this with a conviction that this is the root of the matter. When the Bishop of Assisi said to Francis that his way of life was too harsh and difficult, Francis replied: "My Lord, if we possessed property we should have need of arms for its defense, for it is the source of quarrels and lawsuits, and the love of God and of one's neighbor usually finds many obstacles therein; this is why we do not desire temporal goods." [39]

So many pages have been devoted to the monastic and mendicant orders to make it clear that the Church early realized that those who insisted upon following literally the words of the New Testament must not stop with one or two commandments. Neither perfect poverty, nor peace, nor chastity could be followed by itself. Social life is so intertwined and involved that the only way for a man to follow Christ after the fashion which some sensitive consciences demanded was by such a separation as was possible to monks and mendicants. It is in this light that one must understand the regulations regarding the clergy. Protestant polemics have so centered on celibacy as to obscure the other requirements. It was early taken for granted that a minister of Christ could not use the sword. "I shall be able to grieve, to weep, to groan, against weapons, soldiers, Goths," said Ambrose on an historic occasion to his fearful congregation; "my tears are my weapons, for these are a priest's defense. I ought not, I cannot resist in any other way. . . . . ." [40] And the same Ambrose warned the clergy that they must not engage in business. The only concession was that the clergy might receive an income from their own "little bit of land," if they possessed it. [41] Before celibacy

118

was generally enforced, it was forbidden a priest to contract a second marriage; and Ambrose, indeed, seems to have forbidden all conjugal intercourse to priests.[42] Ministers, like the monks, were to keep the evangelical counsels. But they were to keep them all.

In pacifist references to church history there is little said about the monks or the mendicants. There are, as has been mentioned, numerous references to the Waldenses. This fondness for one medieval group compels some consideration of those sects which held to ascetic ideals. Troeltsch has treated the whole matter from the sociological point of view and has designated as sects those relatively small groups which aspired "after personal inward perfection" and a "direct personal fellowship between the members of the group." It is unnecessary to go into Troeltsch's discussion of the difference between the asceticism of these "sects" and the asceticism of the Church, but it is worth while quoting Troeltsch's summary of sectarian asceticism. It is distinguished by a "refusal to use the law, to swear in a court of justice, to own property, to exercise dominion over others, or to take part in war." [43]

We have knowledge of some withdrawals from the Early Church into voluntary groups professing a rigorous following of the teachings of the New Testament. The most important of these was the Donatist schism in Africa in the fourth century. But it was not until the completion of the hierarchical organization of the Church by Gregory VII (Pope, 1073-1085) that there were groups organized outside

119

the Catholic Church which attracted any widespread following. How numerous these were we do not know. They attracted considerable attention in the eleventh, twelfth, thirteenth, and fourteenth centuries, and we have reason to think that there were numerous sectaries in some localities, for example, in the South of France. The sects are important in church history, but not primarily because of their numbers.

From the beginning of the Church, the opposition between the Church and the world, between the flesh and the spirit, was emphasized until with some it came perilously close to the doctrine of the essential evil of the world and of matter. The great leaders of the Church went to considerable pains to make clear that, while they were exalting virginity, for example, they were not declaring marriage impure or illegal. But there is no mistaking the feeling of some who, like Jerome, denied the essential evil of the body but treated it as if it were. The doctrine of the essential evil of matter was embodied in what is usually called Manichaeism. This was a synthetic religion originating in Persia and laying strong emphasis upon the opposition of good and evil, light and darkness. It had a strong appeal in the Roman Empire, and Augustine was for several years before his conversion a Manichaean. The border line between asceticism and Manichaeism was easily crossed, and provision for a monastic life did not satisfy some.

The most thoroughgoing attempt to separate from the world seems to have been by Neo-Manichaean

120

groups usually called Cathari, or the "pure." Their most important concentration was in Southern France, where they were called Albigenses from their strongholds in Albi.[44] Unfortunately for us, the literature of the sect has almost entirely disappeared, and we are compelled to reconstruct their ideas from the writings of their opponents. But these writings are sufficiently numerous that, making allowance for prejudice, it is possible to trace the history and principal teachings of the sect. The Cathari, or Albigenses, seem to have believed that there are two great principles, the good and the bad. The soul is from the good principle, the body from the bad. There can be no reconciliation between these two, and the height of human blessedness is for the soul to be delivered entirely from connection with matter.

Following out their central doctrine, the Cathari rejected the Old Testament as the record of the work of the evil principle. Thus they cut the knot which had bothered Christians from the beginning. The Old Testament represented God as saying that he would put enmity between the serpent and the seed of the woman. This god of the Old Testament, said the Cathari, is a spreader of discord, while the God of the New Testament is a giver of peace. The New Testament refers to an old saying, that one should love one's neighbor and hate one's enemy. This advice, said the Cathari, is indicative of the nature of the god of the Old Testament, who recommends that we hate our enemy. The Old Testament contained commands to multiply and replenish the earth, while

121

the New Testament says that even looking upon a woman to lust after her is adultery.

It seems that the Albigenses rejected everything connected with the act of generation, refusing to use milk or cheese or eggs. They were vegetarians, making an exception only in the eating of fish, which for some reason they regarded as other than flesh. Marriage is sinful, and it was forbidden to all who had advanced far in the faith. Aside from their abhorrence of the flesh, the Albigenses seem to have thought it wrong to bring children into a world of evil. War was forbidden, even self-defense; and the faithful were not supposed to kill animals or birds. This latter, however, may have been connected with a belief in transmigration of souls. The body was to be subjected by fasting, and suicide by starvation was not unknown among the Albigenses. Under all circumstances oaths in court were forbidden, and the inquisitors used this as a means for detecting the heretics.

The point in referring to the Cathari in this connection is to show how the desire to follow literally the sayings of Jesus expressed itself in a community of believers organized outside the Church. In this case, the group held to a dualistic philosophy which separated them from the main stream of the Christian tradition. Beyond any question the dominance of their doctrines would have been fatal to organized society; but the Cathari only carried to extremes the tendency upon the part of some within the Church to take literally Jesus' sayings, to turn the other cheek, to swear not at all, to receive if possible the saying concerning eunuchs for the kingdom of heaven's sake.

The Waldenses were not Manichaeans. They apparently began with Waldo, a merchant of Lyons. Étienne de Bourbon knew a man who was employed in his youth by Waldo to translate and transcribe the sacred books into the vernacular. Waldo, who did not understand the reading of the Scriptures in the church, had decided to have them translated. When he had read these, along with certain lives of the saints, Waldo decided to seek evangelical perfection as the Apostles had done. Consequently he sold all his goods and gave the money to the poor.[45]

Waldo and his followers began to preach as a result of their having read the Scriptures, but they were forbidden by the ecclesiastical authorities. The Third Lateran Council, in 1179, heard their case, and the pope gave permission for the "Poor Men of Lyons" to preach, provided authority was obtained from the bishop. It seems that in their enthusiasm the Waldenses disregarded this provision, and they were forbidden to preach by the Fourth Lateran Council in 1215.

The Waldenses always claimed to be orthodox Christians and to do nothing but try to form their lives agreeably to the Apostolic precepts. Catholic authorities are agreed that there is no evidence for the scandalous charges brought against them and that their errors were in rejecting the Catholic Church and in insisting upon literal obedience of the evangelical sayings. They would under no circumstances take an oath in court. They would have nothing to do with war. And they held also to the usual abhorrence of such groups for capital punishment. According to Étienne, they believed that judges who pronounced sentence of death were murderers, as were also those who preached that one ought to fight, even against the Saracens.[46] Bernard Gui, an inquisitor in the early part of the fourteenth century, says that the Waldenses did not believe that a Christian should condemn a man even to injury of the body. They based this belief on the words, "Judge not, that ye be not judged." [47]

One other movement should be noticed here. The followers of John Wiclif (c. 1320-1384), commonly called Lollards, held views on poverty and nonresistance similar to those of the Waldenses. Wiclif himself was a scholar and did not personally carry his idea as far as did his followers. He did not forbid the taking of legal oaths, and did not condemn war as always wrong, although he often wrote in what to those unacquainted with the writings of other ages would seem to be "modern" terms.[48] But Wiclif's ideas were developed by his followers into the radical position of those who take the Bible as a code book of laws.[49] He himself was concerned only with the reform of the Church, seeking to restore the ideal of a "poor Church"; but his followers went beyond him, both in their attacks on the Church and in their pacifism.[50]

In the Middle Ages those who sought "naked to

follow the naked Christ" found refuge in monasticism or in the later mendicant orders. Small minority groups were organized outside the Church, although these had little effect upon the course of Christian history. No groups in later centuries could certainly trace their connection with these medieval sects. But whether monks or sectaries, those who fled from the contamination of ordinary life realized the unity of the social order. They believed that they could keep the life of peace only if they abstained from the ties of property and of the family, from civil office as well as military.

Chapter V

THE REFORMATION CHURCHES

THE CHURCH OF THE MIDDLE AGES HAD TRIED TO resolve the tension between the demands of life in society and the literal interpretation of the Sermon on the Mount by providing both for those who would take their part in the ordinary life of their fellows and for those who would practice Apostolic poverty and the other evangelical virtues. The common Christian obeyed the precepts of the gospel, while the monk obeyed both precepts and counsels. Outside the Church small groups tried to apply the teachings of Jesus to the life of every believer, but in so doing they found themselves unable to live in a world of property, courts, and camps.

The changes brought about by the revolt from the Catholic Church in the sixteenth century did not exempt thoughtful Christians from the ancient problem. The Peasants' War in Germany, the Religious Wars in France, the struggles of the Low Countries against Spain—these and countless other smaller contests kept the man of the Reformation period keenly aware of the dilemma which faces anyone who attempts to follow the law of love and at the same time to preserve law and order within a state. Inevitably, each man was influenced by his own conception of the gospel, by his method of interpreting

Scripture, by his beliefs about the nature and powers of the State. Inevitably, too, those Christians who were aware of the long history of the Church and of its thought were influenced by the decisions already made. Over and over again one meets the same statements in regard to the same problems. This is not, however, a sign of sterility of thought, but a tribute to the thoroughness with which the Fathers had considered the fundamental problems of their religion and also a testimony to the unity of the Church throughout the centuries.

The great name of the Protestant Reformation is, of course, that of Martin Luther (1483-1546). He was a bluff and hearty Christian, and it is easy to forget that he was by training, if not by inclination, a monk. In considering his teaching, especially about the Christian way of life, one must bear this in mind, and, along with this fact, the essential inwardness of Luther's religion. For him religion could never consist in outward practices, but in the faith and confidence of the heart. Because he came to believe that the monastic way of life, as he understood it, was not the true Christian way, Luther rebelled against it. In his day, as now, of course, there was endless discussion as to whether Luther was right in contending that men entered the monastery to attain salvation.[1] Luther believed that monasticism was regarded as the road to heaven, a road to be followed by the performance not only of the required precepts, but of the evangelical counsels. His opponents answered, in the usual way, that the monk only took a surer

127

and better road to perfection than that followed by the ordinary Christian. But, regardless of Luther's correctness or incorrectness in this, his attack on monasticism was as important for the Reformation as his assault on Scholasticism and the Papacy.[2]

Luther would have nothing to do with the double morality of the monastic system. He insisted that the Christian law was for everyone, and there could be no distinction drawn between precepts and counsels. To him this distinction was mere quibbling.[3] The Augsburg Confession (1530) represents accurately Luther's reformed views on the subject of the value of the monastic life.

They taught that vows were equal to baptism; they taught that by this kind of life they merited remission of sins and justification before God; yea, they added that the monk's life did not only merit righteousness before God, but more than that, because it observed not only the commandments, but also the counsels of the Gospel. And thus they taught that the monk's profession was better than baptism; that the monk's life did merit more than the life of magistrates, of pastors, and such like, who, in obedience to God's commandment, followed their calling without any such religions of man's making. . . . .[4]

Moreover, they would persuade men that these invented religious orders are a state of Christian perfection. . . . . It is no light offense in the Church to propound unto the people a certain service devised by men, without the commandment of God, and to teach that such a service doth justify men; because that the righteousness of faith, which ought especially to be taught in the Church, is obscured when those marvelous religions of angels, the pretense of poverty and humility, and of celibacy, are cast before men's eyes.[5]

128

Such opinions create false ideas of marriage, of holding property. People

hear celibacy praised above measure; therefore with offense of conscience they live in marriage. They hear that mendicants only are perfect; therefore with offense of conscience they keep their possessions, and buy and sell. They hear that the Gospel only giveth counsel not to take revenge; therefore some in private life are not afraid to avenge themselves; for they hear that it is a counsel, not a commandment. Others do think that all magistracy and civil offices are unworthy Christian men.[6]

Over against all this is set Luther's own doctrine of Christian perfection.

. . . . Christian perfection is this, to fear God sincerely, and again, to conceive great faith, and to trust assuredly that God is pacified towards us, for Christ's sake; to ask, and certainly to look for, help from God in all our affairs, according to our calling; and outwardly to do good works diligently, and to attend to our vocation. In these things doth true perfection and the true worship of God consist: it doth not consist in singleness of life, in beggary, or in vile apparel.[7]

"According to our calling"—in this phrase Luther summed up one of his most important positions. Man was to seek his salvation not in a peculiar religious calling, but in that sphere in which God had placed him. Here he was to live, serving God by the performance of the tasks proper to his station. In his treatise *On the Babylonish Captivity of the Church* Luther advised no man to enter the priesthood or any religious order unless he understood that,

however sacred and lofty may be the works of priests or of the religious orders, they differ not at all in the sight of God from the works of a husbandman labouring in his field, or of a woman attending to her household affairs. . . . . Nay, it very often happens that the common work of a servant or a handmaiden is more acceptable to God than all the fastings and works of a monk or a priest when they are done without faith.[8]

In his calling each man was to live a Christian life, seeking to obey not only the precepts but the counsels of Christ. True, religion is not good works, but faith; nevertheless, the patience, humility, and love of the New Testament, especially of the Sermon on the Mount, are the fruits of faith. They are, indeed, part of the law of Christians.

Give ear now, beloved Christians [writes Luther], and listen to your Christian law. Thus speaks Christ (Matt. 5:39): "Resist not evil. . . . ." Indeed Christ says (Matt. 5:44) that we ought to wish good to those who do us evil, and pray for our persecutors and love our enemies and do good to those who injure us. These are our Christian rights, dear friends. . . . . A child, indeed, would understand from these sayings that it is a Christian law not to resist evil, not to take to the sword, not to defend oneself, not to revenge oneself, but to deliver up one's body and one's possessions, and let anyone take it who will. . . . . Suffering, suffering, cross, cross is a Christian law and there is no other.[9]

It is true that this was written in regard to the Peasants' Revolt when Luther had cried out against the rebels in a way which has forever left a blot on his name. But there is no contradiction in Luther's position concerning the Peasants' Revolt, however much one may wish that he had shown a different spirit. He did not believe that the Christian should raise his hand against the duly constituted worldly powers; and he is stating in the words quoted above the radical doctrine of nonresistance to authority, which he believed to be the rule for all Christians.

But Luther faced, as had all his predecessors, the problem of how a Christian can live in a world of law and government and practice the radical ethic which a literal interpretation of the Sermon on the Mount enjoins. He approached the problem with a doctrine of two kingdoms. There is a Kingdom of God and a Kingdom of this World, and the Christian belongs to both. In the Kingdom of God, there is no sword, no hatred or strife, only mercy and kindness toward one another. But the other Kingdom has been established to restrain, stop, and punish evil. For this reason God has put into the Emperor's hands a sword, not a pen; and the monks who have taught princes to be mild and not to shed blood are wrong.[10] In his earlier period Luther believed that the Christian as a member of the Kingdom of God should not resort to the law for the redress of any injury to himself; but he might go to law to aid his neighbor. As a magistrate or prince, he might use the sword in the prosecution of his duties. Even the hangman is not guilty of blood when he executes a criminal condemned by the courts. Within the Kingdom of God the Christian is to obey the Sermon on the Mount, but this cannot be extended to all society. The results of such an extension would be disastrous; for there are not many true Christians, and society must be protected. The Christian shall be so set himself to suffer evil and injustice without desiring to avenge himself or to protect himself by law, that he most certainly will not need worldly power and law for himself. But for others he may and should—as a judge, executioner, or soldier—seek revenge, law, protection, aid, and in that capacity do whatever he can. Thus authority will also help and protect him, whether of itself, or through the acts of others, but without any complaint of his own. When this does not take place he must let himself be accused and despised, and " 'resist not evil,' as Christ has taught us." [11]

His earlier position, then, was that the Christian might take advantage of the power of the State to redress wrongs done to him only if the help came from the State without his complaint or request. All the Christian could do was passively to accept whatever came—suffering or aid. But if the Christian were a magistrate, then he should enforce the law for others, although not for himself. Later, Luther came to a higher conception of the value of the State. Not that he ever changed his fundamental attitude of passive obedience, but he came to think of the State as not established merely to repel evil, but for positive good. The Christian might then actively co-operate with the State. This is the view expressed in the *Catechisms*. In treating the Fourth Commandment, The Greater Catechism links worldly authority with that of the home.

For here we have not the father of a single family, but the father of as many people as are under him as vassals, citizens and subjects; for God gives to us and preserves to us through them, as through our parents, our food and home, protection and safety. Therefore, since they bear these names and titles as their greatest glory and merit, we also must show them esteem, and honour them as the greatest treasures and most precious jewels on earth.

If one does not obey willingly, but despises this obedience and rebels,

he must know that he will receive neither mercy nor blessing; and if he thinks to obtain one florin by his conduct, he will lose ten elsewhere, or fall a prey to the hangman, or perish through war, pestilence, or famine, or his children will turn out badly, or his household. . . . . Thus according to this commandment we have two fathers appointed: a father by blood and a father by office, or a father of the household and a father of the land.[12]

The Christian as citizen may bear his part in the State.

Concerning civil affairs, they teach that such civil ordinances as are lawful are good works of God; that Christians may lawfully bear civil office, sit in judgments, determine matters by the imperial laws, and other laws in present force, appoint just punishments, engage in just war, act as soldiers, make legal bargains and contracts, hold property, take an oath when the magistrates require it, marry a wife, or be given in marriage. They condemn the Anabaptists who forbid Christians these offices. They condemn also those that place the perfection of the Gospel, not in the fear of God and in faith, but in forsaking civil offices, inasmuch as the Gospel teaches an everlasting righteousness of the heart. In the meantime, it doth not disallow order and government of commonwealths or families, but requireth especially the preservation and maintenance thereof, as of God's own ordinances, and that in such ordinances we should exercise love.

133

Christians, therefore, must necessarily obey their magistrates and laws, save only when they command any sin; for then they must rather obey God than men. (Acts 5:29.) [13]

The Christian cannot make war even against the Turks in order to compel them to be Christians. Our weapons are not carnal, and there can be no holy war. But the Christian can make war when he is acting under the orders of his sovereign. [14]

It is unnecessary to dwell on Luther's attitude toward a just war. He follows here the well-known lines which had been elaborated since Augustine. Only the prince can make war, and Luther is firm against any right of rebellion to constituted authority. But he had to make some exception when the Emperor seemed about to force the princes who were protecting the Reforming party. But he justified the princes on the ground that the Emperor would be attacking the nation or attempting to interfere with their religion. [15] For the rest, we have the familiar statements: the war must be just; an attempt must be made to maintain peace by the offer of justice and peace; if the subject cannot determine whether the war is just, he may obey his prince without peril to his soul. [16] But Luther's real attitude toward the scourge of war even when the Christian seemed to have justification is expressed in the prayer which he recommended to those who go into battle: "Dear Lord, Thou seest that I have to go to war, though I would be glad not to; I do not build, however, on the justice of my cause, but on Thy grace and mercy. . . . ." [17]

134

Luther was a monk, but John Calvin (1509-1564) was a scholar and a lawyer. And as Luther never entirely outlived his monastic training, so Calvin was always aware of the legal and political aspects of every problem. His great work, *Institutes of the Christian Religion* (issued in completed form in 1559), has precedents for its every position. "In Calvin the historical sense of the humanist, and the spiritual passion of the Reformer are united. . . . ." [18] All this must be kept in mind when studying Calvin's attitude toward war, which is, of course, a part of his total attitude toward human society. It helps to explain why Calvin never felt, as did Luther, the tension between the teachings of Jesus and the duties of men as citizens. To the German Reformer, the duties of civil life which could be undertaken by the Christian under necessity were foreign to the citizen of the Kingdom of God; to the French lawyer, the necessity and advantages of life in organized society for Christians and non-Christians, with its police and punishment, were self-evident.

Calvin agreed with Luther that there is no justification for monasticism as a better way of life. Speaking of ancient monasticism, which he believed to have been pure as compared to contemporary Orders, Calvin wrote:

It seemed a good thing to forsake their property in order to exempt themselves from all earthly solicitude; but God sets a higher value on pious exertions for the government of a family, when a holy father of a family, free from all avarice, ambition, and other corrupt passions, devotes himself to this object, that

135

he may serve God in a particular calling. It is a beautiful thing
to live the life of a philosopher in retirement, at a distance from
the society of men; but it is not the part of Christian charity
for a man to act as if he hated all mankind, withdrawing to the
solitude of a desert, and abandoning the principal duties which
the Lord has commanded.[19]

Calvin was not the man to admire monks. He himself was made for magistracy.

Luther had believed that the State should protect
the true gospel and create conditions favorable to
its use, besides the usual duties which devolve upon
the civil power. Calvin goes beyond this in advocating what is in reality a theocracy. And Calvin had
the advantage that he not only set forth his views in
writing, but he demonstrated their workings in a
city state (Geneva). The State and the Church are
separate, but they both obey one law—the law of
God. They are distinct, but not at variance.[20] Civil
government is designed to "cherish and support the
external worship of God, to preserve the pure doctrine of religion, to defend the constitution of the
Church, to regulate our lives in a manner requisite
for the society of men, to form our manners to civil
justice, to promote our concord with each other, and
to establish general peace and tranquillity. . . . ."
This government is necessary because of man's nature.
To imagine that there can be on this earth a condition
where civil government is not necessary is foolishly
to picture a perfection "which can never be found
in any community of men." [21] There is so much
wickedness among men that it is difficult to restrain

it by all the severity of the laws. To speak, therefore, of doing away with civil polity is "inhuman barbarism." Government is as necessary to mankind as bread and water, light and air, "and far more excellent." [22]

Calvin wants it understood that he does not suggest that the State take charge of religion. The State is to preserve the pure religion, but the determination of what true religion is must be in the hands of the Church. This leaves itself open always to the criticism that the system is no reformation, but a restatement of the Catholic position in the Middle Ages. However, Calvin insists that both Church and State are operating by the law of God. This is set forth in the Bible. Therefore, each can find it there.[23]

The powers that be are ordained of God. They are instituted not as the result of human willfulness, but "of the providence and holy ordinance of God." The work of the magistrate, therefore, is the work of God.[24] Even if the magistrate is of the worst character, he is to be obeyed,[25] although there is the usual exception: we are to obey God rather than man. It is the purpose of the State to promote piety. Laws are preposterous which neglect the claims of God and attend only to the interests of men.[26] This needs to be stressed, for while Calvin did not have in mind what is meant by the Social Gospel, yet he undoubtedly conceived of the State as an instrument in the Christianization of society; and in Geneva he had an opportunity to demonstrate this co-operation of Church and State. Professor Choisy has insisted

137

that Calvin's program for the Church in Geneva was a program of social Christianity in the full meaning of the term.[27] But it seems to me necessary to insist upon Calvin's use of the State for the carrying out of his reforms.

Granted the importance of the civil order in the divine plans, especially in the actual promotion of right living, the answer which Calvin had to make to questions concerning the exercise of the magistrate's and of the soldier's office is obvious. Where Luther hesitated before admitting that Christians could go to law, Calvin has no doubts. He makes clear that he does not approve litigiousness, but he insists that one may use the courts without hatred or a desire to persecute. His description of the model plaintiff and defendant, each coming to present his cause without rancor and prepared to waive his rights rather than to sustain enmity, is an interesting statement of the purpose of courts. But Calvin admitted that "an upright litigator" was rare.[28]

At some length and by consideration of texts in the Old and New Testaments, Calvin considered the problem of the Christian magistrate and the shedding of blood. His primary position is simply that the magistrate executes the judgments of God. "Therefore it is easy to conclude that in this respect magistrates are not subject to the common law; by which, though the Lord binds the hands of men, he does not bind his own justice, which he exercises by the hands of magistrates." [29] And Calvin reminds his readers that magistrates can err on the side of mercy.

He may fall into a mistaken humanity, "which is the worst kind of cruelty"; and he quotes the old saying, first applied to the government of Nerva, "that it is bad to live under a prince who permits nothing, but much worse to live under one who permits everything." [30]

As magistrates or princes are entrusted with power to preserve tranquillity within the nation, so they are to repel those who would plunder a whole district. "For there is no difference, whether he, who in a hostile manner invades, disturbs, and plunders the territory of another to which he has no right, be a king, or one of the meanest of mankind: all persons of this description are equally to be considered as robbers, and ought to be punished as such." [31] As to the silence of the New Testament, Calvin answers bluntly: "No express declaration on this subject is to be expected in the writings of the apostles, whose design was, not to organize civil governments, but to describe the spiritual kingdom of Christ." [32] He repeats the saying of Augustine about John the Baptist and the advice to "commiserate our common nature even in him whom they punish for his crime." And Calvin reiterates the advice of all medieval moralists, that every attempt must be made to avoid war, so that no private motive may prevail. [33]

In one thing Calvin's political thinking carries him beyond Luther, who saw the problem of war simply as the question of defending an individual nation. Calvin saw that garrisons, the provision of munitions, and the making of alliances between countries are also legitimatized under the right of war.

The works of Luther and Calvin were largely normative for the Protestant churches in both Europe and America, but the conditions in each country and the personalities of religious leaders modified or expanded the views of the two great Reformers. Opposition, moreover, was very much the same in each country where the Reformation made headway. And on the point in question here the main attacks on the Reformers' position were made by the Anabaptist and similar groups.[34] Their position was that of the Waldenses: the Christian must not take an oath before the magistrate, must not act as magistrate or soldier. As will be seen, there were also some attempts at setting up communistic communities. The Reformed churches, therefore, felt it necessary to express themselves on these points. In England, during the sixteenth century, the religious scene was greatly disturbed by conflicting voices, and the Civil War in the next century released all the divided but pent-up forces in the short period of absolute toleration inaugurated by the Commonwealth. It will serve, therefore, further to illustrate the position of those churches which broke with Rome to quote from the Articles of the Church of England and the writings of a representative nonconforming Puritan, Richard Baxter (1615-1691).

On the points in which we are interested there is little change in the different editions of the Church

140

of England Articles of Religion (the XLII Articles of 1552 and the XXXIX Articles of 1571).

Article XXXVI of the 1552 Articles states that "The civil Magistrate is ordained, and allowed of God: wherefore we must obeie him, not onely for feare of punishment, but also for conscience sake." The 1571 Articles express more carefully the doctrine of the Royal Supremacy. The Article adds: "But that only prerogatiue whiche we see to haue ben geuen alwayes to all godly Princes in holy Scripture by God him selfe, that is, that they should rule all estates and degrees committed to their charge by God whether they be Ecclesiasticall or Temporall, and restraine with the ciuill sworde the stubborne and euyll doers."[35] Concerning war, Article XXXVII of the 1571 recension says: "It is lawfull for Christian men, at the commandement of the Magistrate, to weare weapons, and serue in the warres." It is noticeable that the 1552 Article says "laweful warres," and the Latin version of the XXXIX Articles has "iusta bella."

Article XXXVIII of the 1571 Articles (XXXVII of the 1552) declares the right of Christian men to own property, and Article XXXIX (XXXVIII of the 1552) asserts that the "Christian religion doth not prohibite, but that a man may sweare when the Magistrate requireth, in a cause of faith and charitie, so it be done accordyng to the prophetes teaching, in iustice, iudgment, and trueth."

When we turn to Baxter, the Puritan, we have a more complete discussion of the problem. Baxter has

141

been called a Protestant Schoolman, and he does discuss the minutiae of Christian behavior and doctrine with the thoroughness of the scholastics. Baxter had lived through the Civil War and later was imprisoned by the notorious Judge Jeffreys. No man was more certain of the evils of wars.

> Alas! [he wrote] bloody wars have been more common, and men to men more terrible than mad dogs, or wolves, or tigers. We had sad experience of it in England, Scotland, and Ireland; but other countries have felt much more. They that have not tried it, know not what it is to live under the power of savage soldiers, who domineer over all, and make all slaves to them in their own houses, and keep them under daily fear of death, and take away all they have, and make no more to kill men, than to kill dogs or flies; and if they can but call them enemies, think him the most honourable who killeth most. Oh what dismal sights were our fields, covered with the dead, and garrisons stormed, and all countries filled with men-hunters, who took their neighbour's estates and lives for their lawful prey. . . . . Is it not hard to think of such things with patience, much more to see and feel much of them?[36]

Nevertheless, even nature determines that there should be government, since God made man a sociable creature and insufficient for himself. Rulers are God's officers and receive their power from God. If a man vountarily lists himself under the king's general, the king gives the power to command. If the power is abused, "it is not into the soldier's hand, but into the king's." [37]

Christianity teaches men to live in the love of God and man, to do good to all men as far as they are able, to forbear and to forgive.[38] What then of soldiers? Un-

142

doubtedly the soldier has undertaken a course of life which gives great opportunity to the tempter; "he that never tried it can hardly conceive how difficult it is to keep up piety and innocency in an army." But Baxter is not against the lawfulness of war. For that matter, he did not believe that Erasmus [39] regarded all war as unlawful, although he had much to say about the "horrid wickedness and misery of them that thirst for blood, or rush on wars without necessity." But it is better to be a physician, or a carpenter, or a mason. These save lives instead of destroying them, and build cities rather than burn them. Nevertheless, he would not give the soldiers over as a hopeless sort of men; but, like John the Baptist, Baxter would give them some advice.

In the first place, soldiers should make their peace with God. True, some garrison soldiers live more securely than most men; but the soldier should be ready to die. "He that is fit to be a martyr, is the fittest man to be a soldier." Next, he must be sure that he has "a warrantable cause and call." It is hard to decide what is just, but one must decide either from the "end of the action" or from the authority of the commander. And Baxter observes that, even if a war be unjustly provoked, it may be necessary to fight to prevent the destruction of the king, or country, or religion. But sometimes the sovereign's cause may be good and yet "an erroneous conscience may make the soldier's cause bad." Sometimes the ruler's cause may be bad, but the soldier's good. In case of doubt it is better to remain neutral.

143

When necessity forces one to go into a just war,

do it with such humiliation and unwillingness as beseemeth one that is a patient, a spectator, and an actor in one of the sorest of God's temporal judgments. Go not to kill men, as if you went to a cock-fight, or a bear-baiting. . . . . How unsuitable a work is it to the grace of love! Though I doubt not but it is a service which the love of God, our country, and our rulers, may sometimes justify and command, yet (as to the rulers and masters of the business) it must be a very clear and great necessity that can warrant a war. And, as to the soldiers, they must needs go with great regret, to kill men by thousands, whom they love as themselves.

But, be sure "your cause be better than your lives, and then resolve to venture your lives for them." A coward is one of the most pernicious of murderers, for when men stand to it, there are usually few that die. "If you will be soldiers, resolve to conquer or to die. It is not so much skill or strength that conquereth, as boldness. It is fear that loseth the day, and fearlessness that winneth it."

For the rest, the soldier should obey his commander, avoid pillage, take heed that his heart be not hardened, flee drunkenness and sensuality. Finally, one should not be puffed up by commands or successes. "The experience of this age may stand on record, as a teacher to future generations, what power there is in great successes, to conquer both reason, religion, righteousness, professions, vows, and all obligations to God and man, by puffing up the heart with pride, and thereby making the understanding drunken." [40]

The Protestant Reformation brought little that is

144

new into the discussion of war. But the Reformers agreed that the Christian life is to be lived in the midst of organized society, not in retreat from it. Luther's doctrine of double citizenship strengthened the power of the State, and German thinking has been influenced by this down to the present. Calvin took a stronger stand as to civil power, and his followers were much concerned with the religious effects of political action. John Knox and Oliver Cromwell were both Calvin's sons in the gospel. But the Reformation writers were oppressed by the spectacle of a warring world, and it was with reluctance that they admitted that a Christian man may sometimes bear arms. Yet they saw no escape from the burden of society: the judge and the soldier alike must do his part, even if, in Augustine's words, he prayed to be delivered from his necessities.

Chapter VI

Anabaptists and Quakers

The church historian is prone to confine himself to the churches which stemmed out of the two or three principal Reform movements: Lutheran, Calvinian, or Zwinglian. But there were almost innumerable small groups and even individuals who at one place or another claimed attention for their religious ideas or actions. Some of these, like the Anabaptists, had some part in the beginning of movements which later grew into importance. Others are interesting in themselves or furnish some background for a group like the Quakers, which has remained influential although small in numbers.

One must remember that the Reformation time was a period not only of religious but of social and political disturbance. Medieval economic and social life was breaking up, and even without the religious Reformation that breakup would have affected deeply the lives of men. In the same way the rise of national states was disturbing the older municipal and provincial governments with their dependence upon each other and upon the Empire. It is unnecessary to forget the essentially religious character of the Reformation to understand that the sixteenth century was a time of revolution which affected the lives of both peasants and kings in almost every area of life.

146

In such times there are inevitably clashes and outbreaks, such as the Peasants' War in 1525, which have both religious and social causes. Also religious movements will arise in submerged groups which often, from the point of view of the dominant classes, seem unbelievably radical. This happened during the period of the Reformation in Continental Europe and in the British Isles. The causes were not all social or economic, of course. The Reformers, Luther and Calvin, had each gone as far in his reformation as his conscience or practical sense would allow. There were those who wished to go further. As has often been pointed out, Luther would allow in the churches only that which was not prohibited in the Bible. Others arose who would have in the churches only that directed by the Bible. There is a world of difference between the two.

We have already glanced at certain heretical sects of the Middle Ages. There were individuals and small groups to be found at almost any time who differed from the Established Church in matters of doctrine or of worship or of both. However, there is little evidence to prove a connection between these groups and those which arose during the Reformation. Similar circumstances produced similar movements, but this is about all that can be said. Historians of mystical movements would like to trace relations between, say, the Waldenses and the Anabaptists, but the evidence is inferential.

Our present interest is with those groups which attempted to observe literally the commandments of

147

Jesus. The urge, "naked to follow the naked Christ," as we have seen, has been present at all times in Christian history. Its main manifestations hitherto had been in the monastic orders and in the sects of the Middle Ages. Since the attack of the Reformers centered, among other things, upon the whole monastic system, there was left in Reformed countries only small groups, corresponding to the medieval sects, for the expression of this ideal.

During the sixteenth and the early part of the seventeenth centuries, the best-known group, outside of the main stream of the Reformation churches, was known as Anabaptist. The term was a nickname applied to those groups which believed that the Church is composed of those who have come into it voluntarily and after they have faith. The word actually means rebaptism and refers to the baptizing again of those who had been baptized as children. Although their name refers to baptism, the importance of the different groups lumped together as Anabaptists does not lie in questions of baptism. There were many groups which were called Anabaptists, and it is difficult to distinguish common beliefs; but, on the whole, they accepted the radical interpretation of the Sermon on the Mount and rejected the Catholic system, root and branch.

The name of Anabaptist fell into grave disrepute during the first half of the sixteenth century because of the excesses of certain revolutionaries who departed from the usual nonresistance doctrines of the group and became inflamed with millenarian beliefs. The

classical example was the seizure of the episcopal city
of Münster by John Matthys and John of Leyden and
their followers. It is unnecessary to pay attention to
the scandalous stories told by their opponents, but the
amenities of ordinary life were rough in those days;
and courts at the best were expeditious in dealing out
what was called justice. It is not to be wondered at,
therefore, that the Anabaptists shut up under siege
in Münster were somewhat abrupt in their handling
of those whom they considered enemies. At any
rate, the treatment meted out to the Anabaptists after
the fall of Münster was brutal to the last degree. The
whole story is one of human folly and human cruelty.

But the Anabaptists on the whole were not revolutionaries; so far as we can determine at this distance,
when the surviving documents are mainly from the
hands of their critics, they were simple, law-abiding
people. The movement arose in Zurich among a
number of younger followers of the Reformer,
Zwingli. Among the first movers were several well-
educated men, including Conrad Grebel, Felix
Mantz, and Ludwig Hetzer. Other leaders whose
names are worthy of remembrance were Balthasar
Hubmaier (1480-1528) and Hans Denck (*c.*1495-
1527).

These men were at one in applying Reformation
principles more radically than did the reforming
leaders. They made the Bible the sole authority, rejecting everything that they considered tradition.
They insisted upon adult baptism (the term rebaptism being in their eyes, of course, a misnomer).

149

Their interpretation of salvation was inward, spiritual, sometimes mystical. But they were agreed also that the real Church must be separate from the world and from the governments of the world. They would have none of the Reformers' doctrine of a State which legislated on behalf of the Church. They would obey the powers that be, but only on the principle of passive obedience. In government they could take no active part.

The position of Grebel and the early Zurich group is set forth in a letter which they wrote in 1524. "The Gospel and its followers shall not be guarded by the sword. . . . . They use neither the sword of the world nor war, for to kill is forbidden." [1] In spite of their individual differences in theology and in moral doctrine, Bax seems to be right in saying that the Anabaptists recognized no relation with the State except the duty of obedience.[2] Bullinger, a contemporary opponent, lists among the tenets of the Anabaptists that the Christian should submit and endure the authority of the State; that no Christian can hold public office, or resist evil; that he cannot use the law courts, or kill or punish with imprisonment.[3] The general attitude, then, was that of withdrawal from the world, although there were differences between groups as to the extent of this withdrawal.

Among the moderate Anabaptists were those gathered around Menno Simons (1492-1559), who was born in Friesland. Simons was a priest who in 1536 left the Roman Church and joined the Anabaptists. He drew away from the revolutionary wing and

150

gathered about him the moderates who agreed in the doctrine of nonresistance. Menno believed that no Christian should take an oath, or carry arms, or engage in warfare. Since magistrates compelled men to take oaths and to use the sword, no Christian could be a magistrate.[4] Menno became "the prophet of the type out of which the modern Baptist sects sprang."[5] Through the founders of the modern Baptist movement in England, Menno influenced no little the course of Free Church history.

In England, during the sixteenth century, there are traces of groups holding opinions Anabaptistic in their nature and apparently originating among Dutch emigrants. In a statement concerning various heresies and erroneous opinions put forth in 1530 by an assembly of high-placed churchmen, there is reference to those who believed war unlawful, holding that Jesus Christ

hath not ordeyned in his spirituall kingdom—which is all trewe cristen people—any sworde, for He Himself is the King and governour without sworde and without any outward law. Cristen men among themself have nought to do with the sworde, nor with the lawe, for that is to them nether nedeful nor profitable. The secular sworde belongeth not to Crist's kingdom for in it is noon but good and justice. Criste saith that noo cristen shall resist evil nor sue any man at the lawe.

A form of recantation from an Oxford manuscript of 1575 specifies four "Anabaptistical" errors. Two of them are: "That no christian man ought to be a magistrate, or bear the sword, or office of authority

. . . . That it is not lawful for a christian man to take an oath." [6]

The modern Baptists, however, although the way was paved for them by Anabaptist groups in England, are a separate and distinct movement. They take their origin from some Englishmen who came under the influence of Mennonites in the Netherlands. One of these was John Smyth (d.1612), the so-called "Se-Baptist." Smyth was a Master of Arts from Cambridge, a fine mind and a noble spirit. Having removed to Holland and come under Mennonite influence, he was convinced that he should be rebaptized. He and his companions decided to rebaptize themselves; and Smyth first baptized himself and then baptized his companion, Thomas Helwys, and the others. But, in spite of some peculiarities of belief, there was a broad tolerance in Smyth, and his writings are worth rereading today.

Smyth understood the necessity of government and had no sympathy with the revolutionary Anabaptists, "who take away all rule and authoritie and superioritie among men." If these were taken away, he thought, "then the feare of punishment being abandoned, and the hope of rewards taken away, which are the two Sinewes of the Common-wealth, he [the devil] might easily prostitute men, women, and children to all impious and dishonest behauior: whereby the kingdome of God should be banished out of the world." [7] The "light of nature" teaches that it is better to have a tyrant than no king. According to Smyth,

Magistracie is an excellent meanes to further the kingdome of Christ: and therefore they are compared to nursing fathers and nursing mothers by the Prophet: for as parents doe both beget and bring up children; so godly Magistrates doe erect and maintaine the faith and true religion by the sword: hence it is that the Kings and Queenes of England are intituled Defenders of the Faith: which is the most royall part of the title royall.[8]

Smyth is also sure that a man may "lay up in store for a time to come, and therefore may haue some prouidence and respect to the time to come: for God hath giuen man reason and foresight, which is to be vsed for the preuenting of euill, and the procuring of our good, not only for the soule but for the body also. . . . ." [9] His conclusion is that "couetousnes is a sinne, and so is prodigalitie: liberalitie and magnificence are vertues, so are also parsimony and frugalitie. . . . ." [10] Good men, then, should pray for fruitful seasons; for wise and provident magistrates; for learned and conscionable judges and lawyers; for "Valiant and Christian Captaines and Souldiers, which may resolutely fight the Lords battels against his enemies, such as were the thirtie seauen worthies in Dauids Kingdome"; and for "conscionable and experienced and learned physitions, for the health of the body: and generally all good manuary arts and trades with their skilfull professors, which labour for the preparing of meate, apparrell and their instruments: and in making weapons for warre, &c." [11] It would seem from these statements that Smyth would go on to an acknowledgment of civil duties for Christians. But Smyth said toward the end of his life, in his "Retractations and Confirmations," that he had in all his writings received instruction of others and had been ready to be taught by others. "I professe I have changed," he said, "and shall be readie still to change, for the better." [12] And on the question of Christians participating in civil government, his views did change. In a work printed in 1609, "The Character of the Beast or the False Constitution of the Church," Smyth was uncertain whether a magistrate who was converted to the faith and baptized into the Church could continue his office.[13] But in his "Propositions and conclusions, concerning true Christian religion, conteyning a confession of faith of certaine English people, liuinge at Amsterdam," he had made up his mind.

The magistracy is "a disposition or permissiue ordinance of God, for the Good of mankinde." A magistrate may so please God in his calling that he may bring an outward blessing upon himself, his posterity and subjects. But to be a Christian is too hard for a magistrate. For

if the magistrate will follow Christ, and be His disciple, he must deny himself, take vp his crosse, and follow Christ: he must loue his enemies and not kill them, he must pray for them, and not punishe them, he must feed them and give them drinke, not imprison them: banish them: dismember them: and spoyle their Goods: he must suffer persecution and affliction with Christ, and be slaundered, reviled, blasphemed, scourged, buffeted, spit vpon, imprisoned and killed with Christ: and that by the authoritie of magistrates, which things he cannot possiblie doe, and reteyne the reuendge of the sworde.[14]

154

The members of the church are, moreover, to judge their causes and differences among themselves. They cannot go to law. Neither can they take oaths, but must end their differences by yea and nay. They must not marry "anie of the prophane, or wicked, Godles people of the world." [15]

Smyth's final position was clear, therefore. It was in line with the tradition of all who have separated themselves from the world. He regarded magistracy as ordained of God for the protection of men and even for the advancement of the Church. But Christians could not partake therein. The civil power wielded the sword, and Christian men could not be entangled either in war or in the execution of punishments, not even imprisonments. It would seem that the English General Baptists, who began with a church organized in London by Helwys, a co-pastor of Smyth, held in the main the principles of the Mennonites and those of Smyth. But they showed, as early as 1626, some differences on the question of war. In a correspondence with the Mennonites in Amsterdam, only some of the English Baptists agreed in the nonresistance doctrine of the Dutch churches.[16] The Baptists as a whole were never committed to the doctrine.

The most important of the groups which taught nonresistance in the seventeenth century was the Society of Friends, or Quakers. The character of their founder, George Fox (1624-1691), whose *Journal* is one of the most fascinating of religious autobiographies, their testimony against slavery and

155

war, and the notable contributions of the Society in social work down to the present time, have made the Friends far more important in modern religious history than their numbers would have justified. Largely through William Penn (1644-1718), founder of Pennsylvania, the Quakers became a small but important body in the American Colonies.

The Quakers held to a semimystical doctrine of regeneration and inward illumination. Their relation to the mystical streams in sixteenth- and seventeenth-century England has been the subject of several able studies, especially by Professor Rufus M. Jones. The teachings of the Quakers concerning the inner light do not concern us here. It should be said that the moral principles to which they adhere are derived from their fundamental conception of the Christian life. The Quakers have never admitted that pacifism is a central doctrine with them; their attitude toward war is to them a natural corollary of their total conception of Christianity.

There was a strong note of perfectionism in the early Quakers. Robert Barclay (1648-1690), their first theologian, sets forth, in his "Propositions," that Christians may attain to perfection, although it is a matter of growth. Nevertheless, one may attain in this life a perfection which is such "an increase and stability in the truth," that there cannot be a total apostasy from it.[17] The general tenor of Fox's preaching was to call people out from the world to a community of pure Christians.

156

But with and by this divine power and Spirit of God, and the light of Jesus, I was to bring people off from all their own ways, to Christ, the new and living way; and from their churches, which men had made and gathered, to the Church in God, the general assembly written in heaven which Christ is the head of: and off from the world's teachers, made by men, to learn of Christ, who is the way, the truth, and the life. . . . . And I was to bring people off from all the world's religions, which are vain; that they might know the pure religion, might visit the fatherless, the widows, and the strangers, and keep themselves from the spots of the world. . . . .[18]

The scope of Fox's protest against the manners and morals of his times is summed up in his *Journal* in an entry for 1649.

About this time I was sorely exercised in going to their Courts to cry for justice, and in speaking and writing to judges and justices to do justly; and in warning such as kept public-houses for entertainment that they should not let people have more drink than would do them good; and in testifying against their wakes or feasts, may-games, sports, plays, and shows. . . . . In fairs, also, and in markets, I was made to declare against their deceitful merchandise, and cheating, and cozening; warning all to deal justly, to speak the truth, to let their Yea be yea, and their Nay be nay; and to do unto others as they would have others do unto them; and forewarning them of the great and terrible day of the Lord, which would come upon them all. I was moved also to cry against all sorts of music, and against the mountebanks playing tricks on their stages, for they burthened the pure life and stirred up people's minds to vanity. I was much exercised, too, with school-masters and school-mistresses, warning them to teach their children sobriety in the fear of the Lord. . . . . Likewise I was made to warn masters and mistresses, fathers and mothers in private families, to take care that their children and servants might be trained up in the fear of the Lord. . . . .

But the black earthly spirit of the priests [by which Fox usually means the Puritan, Presbyterian, Congregational and Baptist divines occupying most of the pulpits during the Commonwealth] wounded my life; and when I heard the bell toll to call people together to the steeple-house, it struck at my life; for it was just like a market-bell, to gather people together that the priest might set forth his ware to sale.[19]

These passages are quoted somewhat at length, for they sum up much of Fox's preachings on practical duties. He was also instant against worldly honors and titles and social forms.

When the Lord sent me forth into the world, He forbade me to put off my hat to any, high or low; and I was required to Thee and Thou all men and women, without any respect to rich or poor, great or small. And as I travelled up and down, I was not to bid people Good morrow or Good evening; neither might I bow or scrape with my leg to any one. . . . .[20]

The Quakers got into considerable trouble over their refusal of what they called "hat-honour," since they would not uncover in court or even before the King. Their insistence upon the use of Thou and Thee they defended upon the ground that the use of the plural, you, was because of pride. They also discarded the usual names for months and days of the week. All these peculiarities they thought warranted by Scripture and the demands of a good Christian conscience. Likewise, in the matter of oaths, the Quakers believed the Christian teaching to be explicit. At the Assize at Lancaster, in 1664, when the Bible was given to George Fox and he was ordered to take the Oath of Allegiance, the Quaker leader responded:

Ye have given me a book here to kiss and to swear on, and this book which ye have given me to kiss, says, "Kiss the Son"; and the Son says in this book, "Swear not at all"; and so says also the apostle James. Now, I say as the book says, and yet ye imprison me; how chance ye do not imprison the book for saying so? [21]

The Quaker witness against war is too well known to need illustration, but Fox's own words are worth quoting. In 1650, he was offered a captaincy in the Commonwealth army. He refused, saying: "I told them I knew from whence all wars arose, even from the lust, according to James's doctrine; and that I lived in the virtue of that life and power that took away the occasion of all wars." [22] In 1654, Fox wrote to Cromwell, declaring that he "did deny the wearing or drawing of a carnal sword, or any other outward weapon, against him or any man." He added that he had been sent of God "to stand a witness against all violence . . . . and to turn people from darkness to light; and to bring them from the occasion of war and fighting to the peaceable gospel, and from being evil-doers which the magistrates' swords should be a terror to." [23]

The important words of Fox concerning war are: "to bring them from the occasion of war." Fox reminded his hearers that he was trying to remove from men the lusts and strifes out of which wars come. Few Christian leaders have ever supposed that the cure of war is a promise not to fight. The whole thing goes so much deeper than this. And Fox, in line with the authentic Christian tradition, strove to get at the root of the matter in the human heart. But he recognized that so long as men go about their affairs in the way common to all generations of men wars will arise. Therefore, he would have called men out of the world, to deny all worldly honors and to stand apart from the common ways.

Barclay noticed that a belief in nonresistance and a refusal of oaths were nearly always found together in Christian history. After citing authorities, he says:

From hence it appears, that there is so great a connection betwixt these two precepts of Christ, that as they were uttered and commanded by him at one and the same time, so the same way they were received by men of all ages, not only in the first promulgation by the little number of the disciples, but also after the Christians increased in the first three hundred years. Even so in the apostasy, the one was not left and rejected without the other; and now again in the restitution, and renewed preaching of the eternal gospel, they are acknowledged as eternal and unchangeable laws, properly belonging to the evangelical state and perfection thereof; from which if any withdraw, he falls short of the perfection of a Christian man.[24]

The Quakers did not begin with any hard-and-fast theory of the Christian's relation to the State. They protested against abuses, but they saw no reason why a true Christian should not bear office. In 1656, the General Meeting at Balby advised, "That if any be called to serve the Commonwealth in any public service which is for the public wealth and good, that with cheerfulness it be undertaken and in faithfulness discharged unto God, that therein patterns and examples in the thing that is righteous ye may be to

those that are without." [25]   And there are instances
of Quakers being recommended by their fellows as
fit to serve as justices.   In 1659, seven Friends were
actually chosen as commissioners for the militia in
Bristol.   They were concerned as to whether they
should serve.   Fox had no doubts upon this question,
being sure that Friends are dead to carnal weapons.
They should pay taxes to rulers, who are to keep the
peace; but they could not themselves bear weapons.[26]

As time went on, under the strain of persecution
and with increased separation from the customs and
manners of contemporaries, sharing in civil government became less and less possible.   One cannot
imagine a follower of Fox administering oaths in a
court of law or assessing the death penalty.   As
Braithwaite says, a community that is "in active dis-
sent from the world" tends to become a state within
the State.   Inevitably there were dislocations when
men became Friends.   "Accordingly the business of
working side by side with persons of another way of
life was at no time an easy one: sons who became
Friends left their homes, and servants their masters;
soldiers were dismissed from their regiments; justices
were removed from the Bench; the world went one
way and the Quaker community another." [27]

William Penn, however, not only undertook the
government of a colony, but set up that government.
Under his control, there was difficulty about military
co-operation for the defense of the frontiers, and it
was with some tardiness that he undertook the suppression of piracy.   But he does not seem to have

161

shrunk from the ordinary administration of justice.

Penn, indeed, drew up an "Essay Toward the Present and Future Peace of Europe," which anticipated in several respects the League of Nations. He proposed that the sovereign princes of Europe establish a European Diet which would determine rules of international justice. All differences between nations would be referred to this Diet, and if any sovereign prince refused to submit his cause or to accept the decision of the Diet, "all the other sovereignties, united as one strength, shall compel the submission and performance of the sentence. . . . ." [28]

There is an obvious family resemblance in all the groups, medieval or modern, which denied that a Christian can ever be a soldier. Part of this resemblance is in the fact that they were small groups, frequently persecuted. Because they were frequently persecuted, these groups often became the apostles of toleration. Braithwaite quotes John Audland, an early Quaker, as saying:

Force and compulsion may make some men conform to that outwardly, which otherwise they would not do, but that is nothing of weight, their hearts are never the better, but are rather worse, and more hypocrites than before. . . . . Come forth then with spiritual weapons, mighty ones, in the power of the gospel of Jesus Christ . . . . this is the way to bring people to be of one mind in the Truth, this is God's way, this is the way the saints walked in, this is the way we love and desire.[29]

But the interest of these groups in toleration was not necessarily because of their belief in nonresistance. The Baptists, for example, were not pacifists; but they were mighty in the struggle for religious freedom. There is, however, a consistency among both the medieval and the modern sects in their rejection of the world. They did not urge men to deny only the military life. They recognized that the problem of the judge and the soldier, as well as much else in business and government, hung together. Jesus had said, "Swear not at all," as surely as he had said, "Resist not evil." And if the Quakers remembered that he had said also, "Let your speech be Yea, yea; Nay, nay," they were but adding another barrier between them and the world.

With the later history of the Quakers, or with the successors to the Anabaptists, we are not concerned. Most groups learn how to come to terms with the world; and if they maintain their witness in some of the essentials of the original faith, they have done well. Many modern Quakers have become indifferent to the wearing of rings or to the use of "you," but they have maintained their interest in the extermination of war. Few groups have done more for the Western world, and it is with full recognition of their contribution that these lines are written. But the movement in its inception undoubtedly called men out from the world in a more radical fashion than later generations may think wise. And it is with the character of the original movement that this study has to do.

Chapter VII

The Evangelical Movement

OF THE RELIGIOUS MOVEMENTS WHICH HAVE DEEP-ly affected the English-speaking world in the last two hundred years none has been more important than the Evangelical Revival. Begun by Wesley and White-field in the eighteenth century, the movement was influenced by Pietism, which under Francke and Spener leavened orthodoxy in Germany. The Evangelicals in England were of two schools: the Arminians, who followed Wesley and separated into The Methodist Church, and the Calvinists, who were children of Whitefield and remained as the Evangelical group of the Church of England. But the influence of these two groups has not been confined to the churches to which they belonged or the one which Wesley founded. "We are all Methodists now," wrote an Episcopal clergyman recently, although not with approbation. And the Evangelicals left their imprint especially upon America, where theology was moderated and evangelistic zeal inspired in the various free churches which make up the bulk of American Protestantism.

Controversies concerning the social effects of Evangelicalism have been frequent in recent years. Social historians like the Hammonds have seen in the Evangelical movement a retreat from the world and a substitution of inward piety and otherworldliness for interest in the pressing problems of the present. They have emphasized—some would say overemphasized—the conservative character of the Evangelicals, and have regarded the whole movement as retarding social progress. Others have, of course, as wholeheartedly defended the movement as producing the pioneers of social reform in England and America. The truth is perhaps with neither school of critics. The Evangelicals were, on the whole, conservatives in politics. They had little influence socially until the gradual growth of the Evangelicals in the Church of England gave them political power. Their leaders, such as Wesley and the Seventh Earl of Shaftesbury, were by birth and training gentlemen and not prejudiced in favor of democracy. The Methodist Conferences in England were composed of preachers and were notably conservative in their sympathies.

On the other hand, Wesley and his followers combated with unrelenting zeal the social evils of their day. True, they did not understand the economic consequences of the Industrial Revolution, the effects of which could hardly have been evident to men most of whom died before Watt's steam engine had become much more than a toy. Recent research in English economic history would seem to make it clear that the economic evils of the early nineteenth century were all present in the eighteenth, and against these the Wesleys directed their efforts. It is hardly fair criticism to condemn them for not attacking these evils in the terms of a century which they were not to live to see.[1] In the fight against slavery, Wilberforce and certain of the Evangelicals of the Church of England played a leading part, and Shaftesbury was for years the advocate of movements for the relief of the poor and for popular education.

Nevertheless, the Evangelical movement was religious rather than social. There is a sense in which it was part of the individualistic stream of the eighteenth century. Its emphasis was upon personal religion, and its evangelism was fervently directed toward individual conversion. I must therefore agree with Taylor in regarding Leslie Stephen's statement that "the Methodist movement was essentially moral and philanthropic" as a mistake. And Warner leans too much toward this view.[2] Wesley conceived of his mission as that of "spreading scriptural holiness throughout the land." He saw his task as that of preaching true religion, "Christ in you the hope of glory, Christ reigning in your heart and subduing all things to Himself"; and this religion was the religion which "Kempis, Pascal, Fénelon enjoyed." To be saved means

that the moment a man receives faith . . . . he is saved from doubt and fear, and sorrow of heart, by a peace that passes all understanding; from the heaviness of a wounded spirit, by joy unspeakable; and from his sins, of whatsoever kind they were, from his vicious desires, as well as words and actions. . . . . By salvation I mean, not barely, according to the vulgar notion, deliverance from hell, or going to heaven; but a present deliverance from sin, a restoration of the soul to its primitive health, its original purity; a recovery of the divine nature; the renewal of

166

our souls after the image of God, in righteousness and true holiness, in justice, mercy, and truth.[3]

Holding that religion is of the heart, Wesley also
believed in the necessity of the Church and in good
works. It is not necessary here to enter into a discussion of Wesley's place in the history of Christianity, whether he was a reviver of Luther's doctrine
of justification by faith or whether he was in reaction
toward Catholic positions.[4] But, whatever Wesley's
own intentions, his followers emphasized mainly an
inward experience, that is, religion as personal acceptance, assurance, and peace. The Evangelical
movement did not necessarily mean only gathered
churches composed of adult members, as in the case
of the "sects." The Methodists retained something of
the church organization which they had inherited
through Wesley, while the Evangelical party remained in the Church of England.

There was much talk of withdrawing from the
world among the Evangelicals, but this referred to
customs and habits, particularly in the field of amuse-
ments, which were regarded as unfit for a Christian.
The puritanic features of Evangelicalism which have
occasioned so much controversy were a strong Sab-
batarianism, a distaste for plays and games, and a dislike for ostentation or costliness in dress. But it
should be emphasized that this otherworldliness is far
from monastic asceticism or from the evangelical
poverty of the medieval and later sects.

In plainness of dress, as well as plainness of speech,
Wesley thought the example of the Quakers worth

following. But he did not advise following the Quakers "in those little peculiarities of dress which can answer no possible end but to distinguish them from other people. To be singular, merely for singularity's sake, is not the part of a Christian." He did advise the wearing of inexpensive clothing, "grave, not gay, airy, or showy." "Wear no gold, (whatever Officers of State may do; or Magistrates, as the ensign of their office), no pearls, or precious stones." "Buy no velvets, no silks, no fine linen, no superfluities, no mere ornaments, though ever so much in fashion." There is good scriptural basis for this, thought Wesley; and, besides, the amount saved in wearing inexpensive clothing can be given away. If those who observe the scriptural injunctions "employ the money they thus save in the most excellent manner, then a part of what before only served to fat a few rich tradesmen for hell, will suffice to feed and clothe and employ many poor that seek the kingdom of heaven." [5]

As to plain speech, Wesley understands it to mean the truth without adornments of jest or useless compliments. He was not interested in the "thou" and "thee" of the Quaker.

Alas, my brethren! [he wrote to the Quakers] know ye not, that your ancestors designed this only as a specimen of plain language? And is it possible that you should mistake the sample for the whole bale of cloth? Consult the light God has given you, and you must see that "plainness of speech" does not lie in a single point, but implies an open, undisguised sincerity, a childlike simplicity in all we speak. I do not desire you to refrain from saying *thou* or *thee*. I would not spend ten words about

168

it. But I desire you, whenever you speak at all, to speak the truth, and nothing but the truth. . . . . This is truly plain language.[6]

There can be no better illustration of what Wesley meant by being called out of the world than his doctrine of the use of money. His principle, "Gain all you can; save all you can; give all you can," is famous; but it can be misunderstood unless his comments on it are remembered. The Christian, said Wesley, must not enter into any employment for gain which will impair his constitution. He must not gain to the hurt of his mind. This precludes trade that depends upon smuggled goods, or requires cheating or lying. One must not lose his soul to gain money. The Christian must not engage in any trade or business which hurts his neighbor. This excludes gaming, exorbitant bills, pawnbroking, price-cutting. It forbids distillers or sellers of liquor, unethical or selfish "surgeons, apothecaries, or physicians," who play with men's lives to enlarge their gains. Christians must have nothing to do with "taverns, victualling-houses, opera-houses, play-houses, or any other places of fashionable diversion." Outside of such employments, the Christian should gain all he can by honest industry. By spending nothing on the pride of life, on delicate food or gay or costly apparel, either for himself or his children, he may save in order to give. Wesley would have nothing to do with a tenth, or a third, or a half: the Christian was to give all above his actual necessities.[7]

As to the State, Wesley seems never to have raised

a question concerning the necessity of organized society or of Christians taking part therein. In his "A Word to a Freeholder," he gives advice about voting, warning against bribes and urging that the voter act "as an honest man, a loyal subject, a true Englishman, a lover of the country, a lover of the Church; in one word, a Christian." "Act," he advised, "as if the whole election depended on your single vote, and as if the whole Parliament depended (and therein the whole nation) on that single person whom you now choose to be a member of it." [8]

Wesley was by training and inclination a Tory. He believed that the interests of the King and of England were one and the same. He wrote a tract on "How far is it the duty of a Christian Minister to Preach Politics?" But his message was that the minister should usually preach religion, not politics, unless the King were censured. In that case the minister should preach politics in so far as is necessary "to confute those unjust censures." [9]

He was not sympathetic with talk about liberty of the eighteenth-century sort. Power, he thought, did not reside in the people, and all that was needed for good government could be gained without extending the franchise. A man who had suffered, as had Wesley, from mobs was not likely to be impressed with the demand for political power to be put into the hands of every English male over twenty-one. But his own opinions on government are not of interest here. The present concern is only with those attitudes concerning society which were characteristic of the Evangelical movement.

As to courts, Wesley seems to have taken them for granted as part of the normal structure of government. He interpreted the reference to the sword of the ruler in Romans 13:4 as "the instrument of capital punishment which God authorizes him to inflict." [10] In his sermon on "The Great Assize," delivered at the assizes held before Sir Edward Clive, "one of the Judges of his Majesty's Court of Common Pleas," in St. Paul's Church, Bedford, in 1758, Wesley refers to the office of magistracy.

And, first, how beautiful are the feet of those who are sent by the wise and gracious providence of God, to execute justice on earth, to defend the injured, and punish the wrongdoer! Are they not the ministers of God to us for good; the grand supporters of the public tranquillity; the patrons of innocence and virtue; the great security of all our temporal blessings? And does not every one of these represent, not only an earthly prince, but the Judge of the earth? . . . . O that all these sons of the right hand of the Most High may be as holy as He is holy! wise with the wisdom that sitteth by His throne, like Him who is the eternal Wisdom of the Father! no respecters of persons, as He is none; but rendering to every man according to his works; like Him inflexibly, inexorably just, though pitiful and of tender mercy! So shall they be terrible indeed to them that do evil, as not bearing the sword in vain. So shall the laws of our land have their full use and due honour, and the throne of our King be still established in righteousness.[11]

Here is justice as one of the attributes of God. It might be worth noting that Christians who believed in the Final Judgment, as Wesley unquestionably did, who subscribed to a belief in the moral order of the universe guaranteed and maintained by God, could hardly fail to believe in his justice as well as his love. And it was from this idea of the justice of God that men went on to the idea of justice on earth. To establish that justice Wesley believed the one thing necessary was to have godly men as rulers in the State.

Unquestionably this is both the weakness and the strength of the social teachings of the Evangelicals. They insisted upon the right kind of men in responsible office as absolute prerequisite to good government. Consequently Wesley advised voters to vote only for righteous men.[12] He was not interested in the machinery of reform, although it must be remembered that the burning questions of franchise reform and labor conditions were only beginning to be agitated. One cannot say, however, that he would have thought differently if he had lived fifty years later. Many of his followers did not. That good government is not usually the work of evil men is a truism which can easily be forgotten. But undoubtedly it is not enough. The Evangelical movement stopped short of a satisfactory political philosophy.

Wesley's humanitarian instincts revolted against war. No one has written more bitterly about its conduct and its hypocrisies; no one has more graphically caricatured its "glories."

But there is a still greater and more undeniable proof [he wrote] that the very foundations of all things, civil and religious, are utterly out of course in the Christian as well as the heathen world. There is a still more horrid reproach to the Christian

172

name, yea, to the name of man, to all reason and humanity. There is war in the world! war between men! war between Christians! I mean, between those that bear the name of Christ, and profess to "walk as he also walked." Now, who can reconcile war, I will not say to religion, but to any degree of reason or common sense?

There are causes of war innumerable. Some of the chief are: the ambition of princes, the corruption of their ministers, difference of opinions as to whether flesh be bread or bread be flesh (religious wars), what is the best color or shape for a coat. "There are no wars so furious as those occasioned by such difference of opinions." Two princes may go to war to decide which will dispossess a third of his territory. The strength or weakness of a prince may occasion others to war against him. "Sometimes our neighbours want the things which we have, or have the things which we want." He quotes another as caricaturing the colonial policy of the nations.

Another cause of making war is this: A crew are driven by a storm they know not where; at length they make the land and go ashore; they are entertained with kindness. They give the country a new name; set up a stone or rotten plank for a memorial; murder a dozen of the natives, and bring away a couple by force. Here commences a new right of dominion: Ships are sent, and the natives driven out or destroyed. And this is done to civilize and convert a barbarous and idolatrous people.

But whatever the cause, Wesley would consider the stark fact of war.

Here are forty thousand men gathered together on this plain. What are they going to do? See, there are thirty or forty thousand more at a little distance. And these are going to shoot

173

them through the head or body, to stab them, or split their skulls, and send most of their souls into everlasting fire, as fast as they possibly can. Why so? What harm have they done to them? O none at all! They do not so much as know them. But a man, who is King of France, has a quarrel with another man, who is King of England. So these Frenchmen are to kill as many of these Englishmen as they can, to prove the King of France is in the right.

Meanwhile, says Wesley, we gravely talk of the "dignity of our nature." Men can never be allowed to be reasonable creatures so long as there is war in the world.[13]

Nevertheless, the sufficient answer to the question as to whether John Wesley believed it ever right for a Christian to take up arms is in his letter to the Honorable James West, Member for St. Albans and Joint Secretary to the Treasury, March 1, 1756. The occasion was an expected invasion by the French. The letter speaks for itself.

SIR,—A few days since, Mr. Whitefield and I desired a friend to ask your advice, to whom it would be proper to make an offer of raising a company of volunteers for His Majesty's service. We apprehended the number would be about five hundred. Finding Mr. Whitefield has since been persuaded that such an offer is premature, I am constrained to make the following independently of him:

To raise for His Majesty's service at least two hundred volunteers, to be supported by contributions among themselves; and to be ready in case of an invasion to act for a year (if needed so long) at His Majesty's pleasure; only within . . . . miles of London.

If this be acceptable to His Majesty, they beg to have arms out of the Tower, giving the usual security for their return, and

174

some of His Majesty's sergeants to instruct them in the military exercise.

I am now hastening to Bristol on account of the election, concerning which I wrote to my brother last week; but if my return to London would be of any service, you may command, sir, Your obedient servant.[14]

It must be remembered that the threatened invasion was the more dreaded in England because to the average Englishman it was coupled with the dominance of the Jacobites and of Roman Catholicism. In 1745 the Young Pretender had actually raised his banner and invaded England; and without accurate means of determining public sentiment, the danger of a Restoration seemed to many very great. Charles Wesley apparently did not take very seriously his brother's proffer of volunteers, but he wrote a number of poems on the prospect of invasion which showed that he took that seriously enough.[15]

When the American troubles seemed to be developing into war, Charles wrote to Thomas Rankin in America: "Private Christians are excused, exempted, privileged, to take no part in civil troubles. We love and pray for all with a sincere and impartial love." [16] And the hymns of Charles seem in general to bear out his words. He does not, indeed, appear to have doubted the right of the Christian to fight, but he cannot forget the pity of the slaughter, even in victory. A Thanksgiving was appointed for November 20, 1759, because of a victory over the French fleet. As usual, Charles was ready with a list of hymns. One of them is worth quoting, not be-

cause it is good poetry—it is not even a good hymn—
but because it breathes a Christian spirit, while it
gives thanks for an English victory.

> While Britain's sons their trophies raise,
> Triumphant, as in full success,
>   And bliss without alloy,
> Let pity for our bleeding foes,
> Let love, which no distinction knows,
>   Correct the general joy.
>
> Our country saved from sword and fire
> Doth every Briton's thanks require,
>   And lifts our hearts to God;
> But can we, Lord, delight to see
> These scenes of human misery,
>   This waste of Christian blood?
>
> We mourn the slaughter'd sons of Gaul,
> We tremble, while Thy judgments fall
>   On our invaders' head:
> Their lives to ransom ours are given,
> And crowds out of the body driven
>   Have perish'd in our stead.
>
> .   .   .   .
>
> Saviour of men, through whom we live,
> Do Thou the peaceful answer give
>   While at Thy feet we groan:
> Stop this effusion of our blood,
> Thou who hast quench'd the wrath of God,
>   By pouring out Thine own.
>
> Repentance upon both bestow,
> Our foes and us; that each may know
>   Their sins through faith forgiven,
> That all may cordially embrace,
> And sweetly reconciled by grace
>   Go hand in hand to heaven.[17]

Among the Evangelicals of the Church of England in the nineteenth century, Anthony Ashley Cooper (1801-1885), Seventh Earl of Shaftesbury, was outstanding both for his devotion to Evangelical principles and for his work as a social reformer. Shaftesbury's evangelicalism was of a narrow and unyielding character, and he has made little appeal to Churchmen and reformers of other schools, either in his own day or at the present. The Hammonds have handled him somewhat roughly in emphasizing the rigidity of his moral and religious views, but they acknowledge his social contribution. "He did more than any single man, or any single Government in English history to check the raw power of the new industrial system." [18] Such is their judgment. And in the *Encyclopaedia of the Social Sciences*, J. L. Hammond says that Shaftesbury "did more than any single man to give a new tone on social questions to the upper-class world of his day." [19]

Shaftesbury was in Parliament, either in the House of Commons or in the House of Lords, from 1826 until his death, with only one interlude when he resigned because he changed his mind as to the corn laws. He refused political preferment and devoted himself to unpopular causes in favor of the working classes. He was a leader in legislation to take young women and children from the mines, to secure a Ten Hours Act, housing reform, and to stop the employment of chimney sweeps. His educational work was largely in connection with schools for the poor, known as the Ragged Schools. He was a Tory

177

by birth and sympathies, as were many of the Church of England Evangelicals. As a Tory he was possibly moved somewhat by opposition to the newly arrived factory owners and entrepreneurs. But he was also, because of his position and politics, able to use political power for reform. The Methodist and Dissenters, as a whole, were more often Liberals; and their direct influence on Reform was through their desire for participation of the lower classes in government, a desire which was by no means shared by Tories, Evangelical or otherwise.[20]

Shaftesbury counted himself an Evangelical of the Evangelicals, and he considered John Wesley one of the greatest figures in church history. He was in the line of the "Evangelical succession" and participated both in the good and the bad of that party. He was a strict Sabbatarian, although he contended not only for Sabbath relief for workers but also for the half-holiday on Saturday. He was a Protestant inclined to view everything Catholic with suspicion, but he supported the Catholic Emancipation Act. He was a loyal member of the Church of England, but he worked for the Religious Liberties bill, allowing freedom of worship, which was much restricted in the first part of the century.

As a member of Parliament, Shaftesbury naturally had no feeling that Christians should avoid governmental responsibilities. "He believed that morality could be expressed in political terms: What is morally right can never be politically wrong, and what is morally wrong can never be politically right." Bready

178

has properly emphasized Shaftesbury's view that law is not only to repress evil but "to enlarge man's freedom." Indeed, Bready believes that Shaftesbury changed the legislative outlook among English-speaking peoples "from political to social." [21] Holding such views, Shaftesbury naturally proceeded from his Evangelical principles to oppose the abuses which he believed to be morally wrong. This explains his opposition to such evils as slavery and the housing conditions of the poor, and partly, at least, accounts for his lack of interest in what he regarded as purely political reforms, such as the extension of the franchise.

Throughout his life Shaftesbury was opposed to militarism. One almost hears an echo of Wesley in Shaftesbury's comment after visiting the naval station at Portsmouth. "If the nation would show one-half the zeal to defend itself from the devil that it does from the French, we would speedily become a wise and impregnable people." The conduct of his countrymen abroad did not escape his censure. "Grand battles by the Indian mail," he wrote in 1843, "grand victories, and still grander injustice! Wrong and robbery on a splendid and successful scale are sure to be hushed up, if not applauded. I shrink with a combined feeling of terror and nausea from our national sins."

But when the French established a protectorate over Tahiti, Shaftesbury saw in this a threat to the missionary work which had been carried on there.

179

Grief and indignation cannot go beyond what I feel against the French aggression in Tahiti. A peaceable and helpless people, a State presenting, as such, the only Christian model in the world, are subjugated by savages and powerful Europeans, and inundated with bloodshed, devastation, profligacy, and crime. God gave the regeneration of this island to our people as a triumph of the Cross. . . . . The missionaries made it Christian; they made it English in laws and constitution. . . . . Public men estimate its value by political measurements and the probable effects on their own ease and tenure of office. What a disgusting and cowardly attitude for England, thus to stand by and not raise a hand in defense of this merciful gift of Providence! [22]

Shaftesbury did not say explicitly that England should have gone to war, if necessary, to defend Tahiti; but he was too experienced in public life to imagine that any diplomatic protest not backed up by military power would have been of any avail. In the Crimean War he spoke plainly. As between Russia and Turkey, although he called the Turk insane and the Muscovite wicked, Shaftesbury had no hesitation in making a choice. When the Czar declared that England and France had ranged themselves by the side of the enemies of Christianity against Orthodox Russia, Shaftesbury was chosen to address the House of Lords in reply. In his speech he insisted that Russia had done everything to retard the progress of Christianity, while in recent years Turkey had done everything to advance the cause. He thought that England could not do anything else but make "alliance with any power, heathen though it may be, to maintain the cause of right, justice, and order, against the aggressions even of professing Christians."

His native shrewdness led him to advise watching France, although the Emperor had "acted wonderfully well." Indeed, the Emperor had declared that the days of conquest are past, and that the repression of Russia was necessary for the sake of civilization. "It would be wrong, nay, unjust, to suspect him; to have even a misgiving; and yet the change is so immense, his policy so unexpected, that one ought, for some time at least, to be upon one's guard."

In the same way Shaftesbury was apparently none too sure even of the English peace party. He quotes without comment, but in a context which indicates his approbation, the "clever" letter which Drummond wrote to the Peace Society, "in which he tells them that they desire peace, only that they may have leisure to make money; that if war would answer the purpose, they would (he implies) like it as well, that they denounce Mars and Moloch, but worship Mammon, who according to Milton, is the basest and meanest of them all!" [23]

Hodder, Shaftesbury's official biographer, comments that "war in a Christian spirit" presented no anomaly to his mind. It was, however, anomalous that any action in war should be undertaken in any but a serious spirit. He felt that soldiers should be sent forth with prayer, and that their victories should be celebrated by giving thanks to God. It is not to be concluded, however, that Shaftesbury was in a haze of warmongering. He was convinced of the justice of England's cause, but he was bitter in his criticisms of the conduct of the war; and he was responsible for organizing and sending out the Sanitary Commission, which Florence Nightingale said saved the British army. Indeed, Miss Nightingale sent the Earl a copy of her report on sanitary matters, because she considered that the work done in Crimea was so largely owing to his efforts.[24]

The attitude of the Evangelicals toward war can very well be summed up in one of Shaftesbury's prayers.

O Lord, Almighty God [so runs the prayer in his diary], protect those gallant men of both nations (England and France) by sea and land, from the pestilence, the battle, and the flood; give them a speedy and joyous victory; a speedy and a lasting peace; restore them safe and happy to their land, and that right soon. We pray not, O Lord, in malignity or revenge, but for the peace of nations, and the security of freedom; restrain the ambition of this man, stay his encroachments, confound his devices, and turn his heart. Rend from him his ill-gotten gains, the acquisitions of fraud and violence, confine him within his own limits of race and language. Save a Protestant land from idolatrous rule, and enable us to do some great work for Poland, of justice, mercy, and retribution; and thus, by Thy grace, both in the East and in the West, Thy word shall have free course and be glorified through Jesus Christ our Lord.[25]

In their attitude toward the State, toward participation in government, and toward war, the Evangelicals were in the line of the dominant tradition from the first century on. They preached separation from the world, but this did not mean leaving government and social order in the hands of non-Chris-

182

tians. Indeed, the Evangelical theory was that good men in office would insure good government, although Shaftesbury and others were quick to attack the slave trade and attempt to regulate factory hours through political means. The Evangelicals were against war, as all Christians, with few exceptions, have been; but they were not pacifists in the modern, absolute sense. They regarded war, again in the line of dominant Christian tradition, as always a calamity but as sometimes the only way to prevent international outrage. Their judgments as to individual cases may have been wrong—English and American writers still differ concerning Wesley's *Calm Address to the American Colonies*—but their principles were historic Christian principles.

Chapter VIII

THE SOCIAL GOSPEL

TO SINGLE OUT THE SOCIAL GOSPEL MOVEMENT TO
stand beside the other phases of Christian history mentioned in this volume may seem to some historically
minded readers an undue emphasis upon one aspect
of Anglo-American Christianity. Logically it might
be better to devote the space to a consideration of
the Liberal movement in theology, but actually it
is not Liberalism but the Social Gospel which con-
cerns this study. The latter had its rise in America
and acquired certain emphases peculiar to this country, but it stands for a development in Christianity
which cannot be ignored, and will possibly not be
lost.

Critics of the Social Gospel have been irritated by
the apparent assumption of some of its advocates
that social interest on the part of the Church is an
innovation.[1] The advocates themselves would doubtless answer that the particular type of social interest
represented by the Social Gospel is an innovation;
and in this they would be correct. In its beginning
the movement combined both the emphasis of medieval Catholic and Genevan Christianity with the
"moral" social program of the Evangelicals. That
is to say, the Social Gospel partook of the nature of
a "reform" movement, which means domination of

184

the individual by the group, and at the same time was evangelical, seeking to reform the world by reforming individuals. This can be seen in a man like Walter Rauschenbusch, the greatest prophet of the Social Gospel in America. Rauschenbusch retained throughout his life a combination of personal regeneration and political-social reform as his goal. "He felt that Christians must change the economic system in order to be able to live with their religious faith, but at the same time must strengthen their religion in order to be able to change the economic order." [2] Throughout his life, Rauschenbusch's position remained essentially the same. He would not take part in a movement which was not led by men with clean hands. At the same time, Rauschenbusch felt that there must be changes in the social order to liberate the possibilities in men.

It is in this idea of the importance of environment for the spiritual life that the Social Gospel in America has, perhaps, made its unique contribution. According to Professor John C. Bennett, "one of the points at which the modern Social Gospel is in advance of earlier Christian teachings is that its representatives have been able to see clearly the ways in which human personality is moulded and often warped by environment, by institutions and economic circumstances." [3] It would not be true to say that the Christian Church was not aware throughout its history of the importance of environment to spiritual life; but there are ways in which the Social Gos-

185

pel differs from the historic Church in its interpretation of the influence of environment.

In the first place, the scientific advance of the nineteenth century equipped men to understand better the influence of material factors in the environment. Food and shelter and recreation became important for their effects upon the mental and spiritual life of men. And the need for mental development was recognized and lay behind the extension of educational opportunities. In addition to the older Christian motive of justice and the humanitarian impulse toward sympathy with the unfortunate, there was scientific testimony to the individual's need for proper material environment. The three historic attitudes which Christians have taken toward an improper environment have been, to flee from it, to bear it, or to try to change it; and the last is characteristic of the Social Gospel.

One can hardly stress too much what in the Social Gospel is owing to the scientific developments of the modern world. The ancient world knew how to bring water to the city; but only after methods of testing that water were developed could men be sure that the water really was pure, and only through modern developments in scientific advance could one know how to purify the water if it were found impure. Further, no doctrinaire theories about the perfectibility of mankind could have convinced the ordinary man that he could have a radically different environment, but it needed little argument to persuade people who saw the rapid technological developments of the latter part of the nineteenth century that there is no limit to the changes that science can make. Literary historians are always liable to overestimate the importance of books. Many a man who never heard of Herbert Spencer was convinced of the perfectibility of mankind because he had electric lights in his house.

I stress this latter point because a good deal has been made of the optimism of America, and much has been said about the derivation of this optimism. Some have thought it came from the frontiersman, while some have traced it to the influence of the Renaissance. As a matter of fact, doctrines concerning the nature of man have perhaps not been so important as the ocular demonstration of changes that could be brought about in environment. After all, the inventor and the businessmen who made that invention a practical, salable object are to be given the credit—or the blame—for most of the optimism of the latter nineteenth century. Men who saw streets paved, houses lighted, sewerage installed, steam trains succeeded by electrical, the automobile owned even by the common man, were sure that any change man wanted could be made. Something must be allowed also for the rapid changes that came about in the experiences of individual Americans. The standard theme of the poor boy who became rich and married the boss's daughter had no little effect on the spirits of Americans for forty years or more. In a country like this anything could happen. I realize that this is not the academic explanation of

187

American optimism, but I think it had a great deal more to do with it than those esoteric causes which are so often assigned.

One must remember, too, that until very recent time it was useless to appeal to the ordinary Christian to help change the environment of himself and his neighbor. He simply had nothing to do with it. Treatises in the Middle Ages directed to the prince are not evidences of the writers' aristocratic tendencies; but it simply helped nothing to address anybody else. The extension of the franchise, therefore, was a necessary prerequisite to any widespread development of a Social Gospel.

It was the rise of the city that caused the Church to turn its attention in any comprehensive way to social problems. It is somewhat silly to denounce the Church of the 1870's and 1880's for not having been absorbed in urban social problems. In 1880 over 71 per cent of the population of the United States were in rural areas. The countryman, to be sure, had social problems enough; but his greatest difficulties were not with other people but with the forces of nature. It was only when large groups of people began to live in cities that modern industrial problems became evident. "Crowded with unassimilable aliens and faced by tremendous social problems, these cities were struggling with lawlessness and crime, tenements, crooked politics, delinquency, sanitation, traffic, inadequate religious resources, and a host of other complexities." [4]

188

And the American churches were ready to enter into a struggle for better conditions. Not much is said about it in tracing the origins of the Social Gospel in America, but it must be remembered that American Protestantism in particular had been stirred to its depths by the antislavery movement. For many years before the Civil War a large section of the churches had been engaged in a life-and-death struggle to eradicate slavery. The story is too well-known to be repeated, but it must not be forgotten that with the end of the Civil War a tremendous reservoir of moral enthusiasm remained unexhausted. To understand the nature of this enthusiasm, Julia Ward Howe's famous song is instructive. Some of the stanzas of the "Battle Hymn of the Republic" are:

Mine eyes have seen the glory of the coming of the Lord;
He is trampling out the vintage where the grapes of wrath are
  stored;
He hath loosed the fateful lightning of His terrible swift sword;
    His truth is marching on.

I have read a fiery gospel, writ in burnished rows of steel:
"As ye deal with my contemners, so with you my grace shall
  deal;
Let the Hero, born of woman, crush the serpent with His heel,
    Since God is marching on."

He has sounded forth the trumpet that shall never call retreat;
He is sifting out the hearts of men before His judgment seat;
Oh be swift, my soul, to answer Him! be jubilant, my feet!
    Our God is marching on.

This is, of course, the Holy War, although many of the Fathers and Doctors of the historic Church would have been reluctant to say that the grace of God is given in proportion to success in battle. But the point is that the reforming tradition in America was militant.

In other ways, too, the American Protestant churches were prepared for the Social Gospel. They were most of them evangelical in doctrine and evangelistic in practice. So nearly were they alike in the essentials of faith that they had overcome the separatist tendencies of Protestantism sufficiently to enable them to work together in evangelistic effort, in temperance campaigns, and later in such organizations as the Y.M.C.A.

But the Social Gospel became more than a reform movement. Visser 't Hooft insists that it is "more than an application of Christian principles to society; it is also an application of social principles to Christianity, or to put it shortly: it is a form of interpenetration of religious and social thought."[5] This is true. No matter how orthodox the motive and character of the Social Gospel, it soon implied assumptions which are new in the history of the Christian faith. To some extent, at least, the comment of a famous church historian on a popular preacher of the new type, twenty-five years ago, was justified: "What he preaches," said the historian, "is interesting; it may be true; but it isn't Christianity." This is not the place for a discussion of the theology of the Social Gospel, and it will be mentioned only where

190

it is necessary for this study. But it is important to note that this theology is not simply a product of the "inter-penetration of religious and social thought"; neither is it merely a survival of Renaissance influence. The spirit of the times in this country set the stage and determined in part the course of the movement, and certain developments in thought and action were ready to hand.

America was on the make. In the latter decades of the nineteenth century and the first decades of the twentieth, nothing seemed improbable. Painstaking efforts have been made to point out how thoughtful men and women foresaw ruin ahead; but the pessimists were, in their way, just as optimistic as the optimists. Ruin was ahead—unless their particular reforms were adopted. One writer has said that the bitterness of American humor in the middle of the nineteenth century was owing to the fact that somebody had at last got to the Pacific Ocean and people knew that there was an end to the free land possible in America. This is certainly going far to explain American humor which is of a piece with that of Benjamin Franklin. Certainly there were social thinkers who understood that the conditions developing in the newly industrialized urban districts would bring on problems that must be settled. But with few exceptions, even these thinkers were sure the solution could be found.

At any rate, nobody cared to withdraw from this excellent world. And there was no place in the churches for a preachment of withdrawal either to the desert or to such retreat as certain sects had favored when they refused to be entangled either with property or with the State. Santayana has criticized the churches for so completely cutting off from the past and courting the good opinion of this world.

> Although called evangelical, they were far, very far from prophesying its end, or offering a refuge from it or preaching contempt for it; they existed only to serve it and their highest divine credential was that the world needed them. . . . . Why distract this world with talk of another? Enough for the day was the good thereof. Religion should be disentangled as much as possible from history and authority and metaphysics, and made to rest honestly on one's fine feelings, on one's indomitable optimism and trust in life.[6]

If this seems too harsh, certainly one has to concede that the Church was dealing with what was of greatest interest to everybody—the goods of this present world. No Christian who knew of the social writings of the Middle Ages, who had read Calvin or Wesley or had heard of Shaftesbury, would deny that the Church, in acting in the social sphere, was acting in line with its sound tradition. But one must admit also that, in putting stress upon the Social Gospel to the exclusion of some other elements, the churches were changing the essence of their message.

But they were in line with the tendencies of the time, for reform was in the air. In the early 1900's revolt against social and political evils was common talk. William Jennings Bryan and Theodore Roosevelt dramatized the popular protest against unjust combinations, "trusts," and the accumulated evils of rapidly growing industrialization. The cartoonist represented the "common people" as a half-dazed, innocent victim of the machinations of myriad sinister interests; and even the humorists joined in the outcry: "Here comes property, dhrunk an' raisin' Cain." [7]

The Social Gospel, considered not as the social applications of Christianity but as a reinterpretation of Christian doctrine, or, to use Rauschenbusch's phrase, "the adjustment of the Christian message to the regeneration of the social order," depended also in no small measure upon a new conception of the New Testament. This conception was made possible by the critical work of New Testament scholars in the latter part of the nineteenth century. It is unnecessary to retell here the story of New Testament scholarship as it attempted to discover the historical Christ. But the Social Gospel based its theology on, first, an attempt to rediscover the historical Jesus and, second, the belief that he was rediscovered in his teachings, particularly as they had social meaning. There are, as everyone knows, passages in the Gospels which have to do with the future and which are called the eschatological passages. Obviously, if Jesus expected an imminent end to the world one could hardly believe that he intended his followers to regenerate the social order and establish the Kingdom of God upon earth. But a theory of New Testament scholarship that was at the height of its pop-

193

ularity in America in the latter part of the nineteenth and early decades of the twentieth century, and which is still widely held, seemed to obviate these difficulties. This was the theory that the Gospel of Mark and a lost document which lay behind Matthew and Luke, and which consisted in large part of those portions which are common to both Gospels, were the original documents. Taking Mark and this unknown document called "Q," with some elisions of troublesome passages, one had a remainder which seemed straightforward enough and might be used for a historical story of Jesus that did not too much separate him from the Western mind. Rauschenbusch quotes with confidence Harnack's statement that "the tendency to exaggerate the apocalyptic and eschatological elements in our Lord's message and to subordinate to this the merely religious and ethical elements will ever find its refutation in Q." [8]

This is not to say that no social interpretation was thought possible except upon the basis of this critical position. Shailer Mathews, writing in 1897 a book which was reprinted thirteen times by 1917, laid down certain simple but sound historical principles for the interpretation of the Gospels. One is to distinguish between the teachings of Jesus and the editorial material added to them by their writers. The Fourth Gospel was to be interpreted with care, but many of the passages that are not original there "are self-evident to the careful reader, and most are easily separated from the teachings of Jesus by simple processes of criticism." [9] It would be a brave man today who would think the task as simple as this; but the critical processes to be used by the reader, as Mathews advises, were the processes established in the accepted two-source hypothesis. European critics of the Social Gospel, it is true, point out that American writers have usually treated the eschatological interpretation lightly, if not with contempt. Dr. Charles A. Ellwood, whom Visser 't Hooft particularly cites, does speak of the eschatological interpretation of Albert Schweitzer and others as being difficult for a plain man to understand, and dismisses it simply as German theology.[10] But, as Visser 't Hooft admits, Rauschenbusch was more careful in his statements and realized the difficulties of interpretation. Beyond a doubt, however, some of the more extreme advocates went further. Harry F. Ward, while denying that Jesus was simply an ethical teacher, insists that the characteristic of his religion owes its vitality to its ethical principles; and these, Ward thinks, have always been evident to those who come to the study of the religion of Jesus without the presuppositions of ecclesiastical Christianity.

When for instance Jefferson, the free-thinker, made his own Bible by putting together the ethical sayings of the gospels, when Lincoln said he would join the church that wrote over its doors the fatherhood of God and the brotherhood of man, when Gandhi—heir of another tradition—declares that he owes his passion for bringing separated human beings into fellowship to the Sermon on the Mount as well as to his Hindu scriptures, it is the ethical element in the religion of Jesus that evokes the response.[11]

And this authentic kernel of the teaching of Jesus has little to do with the magic that appears in the story.

> It is the Golden Rule and the Sermon on the Mount that express Jesus to the common people. Those who come to the gospel untrammeled by any of the doctrinal interpretations of ecclesiastical religion are inevitably impressed by their moral challenge. True the element of magic appears in the story, but the scholars tell us that the closer we get back to the actual words of the Galilean the clearer it is that his religion is essentially ethical, that this is the characteristic of the doubly attested sayings which are the most authentic part of the record. It appears that the work of corrupting the simplicity and softening the moral imperative of Jesus began early.[12]

Most New Testament scholars would agree today that this is an oversimplification of the problem, and that the attempt to get back to sayings of Jesus that will cause no difficulty for a modern reader is to do away with the authentic documents themselves.[13]

In the reconstruction of Christian theology for the Social Gospel on the basis of the supposed authentic documents of the New Testament, the principal teaching of Jesus is taken to be that concerning the Kingdom of God, but the Kingdom of God interpreted in a very definite manner. According to Rauschenbusch, it is "humanity organized according to the will of God." [14] "By the Kingdom of God," wrote Mathews several years before Rauschenbusch's book on theology, "Jesus meant an ideal (though progressively approximated) social order in which the relation of men to God is that of sons,

and (therefore) to each other, that of brothers." [15]
And Ellwood puts this even more distinctly.

When he commands his followers to seek first the establishment of the Kingdom of God, this [redemption of all men] is
clearly his thought. For this phrase, at one time perverted by
theologians to a supermundane or even ecclesiastical meaning,
has been shown by modern scholarship on the whole to have
reference to a social order upon this earth—an order, however,
not of mere brotherhood—for brothers may be co-conspirators
in crime—but one in which God is acknowledged as father and
his will is realized through the loving obedience of men to all
his laws, especially to the laws of mutual love, mutual service,
and mutual self-sacrifice for the sake of human service.[16]

To this new interpretation of the meaning of the
Kingdom of God, theological doctrine must be ad-
justed.

Since the Kingdom is the supreme end, all problems of personal salvation must be reconsidered from the point of view of
the Kingdom. . . . . If the Kingdom of God was the guiding idea
and chief end of Jesus—as we now know it was—we may be sure
that every step in his life, including his death, was related to
that aim and its realization, and when the idea of the Kingdom
of God takes its due place in theology, the work of Christ will
have to be interpreted afresh.[17]

And this applies, of course, to the doctrine of God.

A theological God who has no interest in the conquest of
justice and fraternity is not a Christian. It is not enough for
theology to eliminate this or that autocratic trait. Its God must
join the social movement. The real God has been in it long ago.
The development of a Christian social order would be the highest

197

proof of God's saving power. The failure of the social movement would impugn his existence.[18]

None of these writers, Mathews or Rauschenbusch or Ellwood, would exclude the religious element. For that matter, neither would Harry Ward. But the religious element is much more obvious in the first three. And the methods by which the Kingdom of God is to be brought upon earth are, at least with the first three, primarily those methods of fellowship and brotherhood exercised in the family and in all social relations which would affect the larger areas of man's life. But when one presses the question as to the way this dominance of the ideals of Jesus in social life can be brought about, it leads to the consideration of one subject which is not often mentioned in relation to the Social Gospel. It can be seen by examining more closely such a statement as that of Rauschenbusch in regard to the Kingdom of God. He affirms certain convictions about the ethical relations within the Kingdom. "Since Christ revealed the divine worth of life and personality, and since his salvation seeks the restoration and fulfilment of even the least, it follows that the Kingdom of God, at every stage of human development, tends toward a social order which will best guarantee to all personalities their freest and highest development." This involves removing religious bigotry, the repression of self-assertion in the relation of upper and lower classes, and all forms of slavery. Secondly, since love is the supreme law of the Kingdom, the advance of the Kingdom may be seen wherever "the

198

free will of love supersedes the use of force and legal coercion as a regulative of the social order." But this involves redeeming society from political autocracies and economic oligarchies, changing the nature of its penology, abolishing constraint through hunger as part of the industrial system, and doing away with war. Moreover, the highest expression of love is "the free surrender of what is truly our own, life, property, and rights." "No social group or organization can claim to be clearly within the Kingdom of God which drains others for its own ease, and resists the effort to abate this fundamental evil." Finally, the reign of love tends toward the progressive unity of mankind, "but with the maintenance of individual liberty and the opportunity of nations to work out their own national peculiarities and ideals." [19]

But again, how is all this to be brought about? It may be answered that it is by the living of Christian lives, by the creation of public opinion. But certainly Christian lives and public opinion would be useless unless they affected the legal structure of nations. Ellwood carries the matter further in advocating the use of social science. Jesus was not a social reformer and did not have a cut-and-dried formula for a fixed social order. Therefore it is necessary to ascertain "by careful investigation" the needs of men in their economic, political, and intimate social life. "Such investigation must furnish to social religion guidance in all the special problems of human life," and alone "can render values concrete and vital." [20] Ellwood well understands that no revolution in social and industrial organization will remedy, for example, the evils of the economic system. The change must be "climatic." The whole spirit of the business and financial world must be changed. But here, as everywhere in social life, "changes in inner spirit and aim must be accompanied by changes in external methods and order if any lasting betterment is to be effected." [21] In the same way, Ellwood recognizes the necessity of a change of spirit in our political life. This end must be sought through the highest and best development of each nation. Such politics, he contends, are not inconsistent with the highest patriotism, and "patriotism and humanitarian religion may in time thus blend and become practically indistinguishable, though at present they may so often seem to be in contradiction to one another." [22]

Obviously what is understood in these discussions is the use of political means to achieve the external changes necessary, although none of these writers would suggest that the external changes are in themselves enough.

Harry Ward is more specific. He says of American Protestants that

they are politically powerful enough if they choose to do it to turn their country from its present tendency to become the center and support of world reaction by its defense of antisocial forms of property. They can lead it to play a significant part in shaping the Great Society by dedicating its resources and technical skill to a general plan for the common well-being of mankind.[23]

If they fail to do this, he thinks that their religion

200

will become another cult of aesthetic or rationalistic escape.

What has emerged, then, is not simply a new theology, but a very definite doctrine of the relation of the Christian to the State. And this doctrine is unquestionably that of the Christian's participation in the activities of the State to the fullest extent possible within the limits of his convictions. In a democratic country, public opinion crystallizes in the ballot box; and it is assumed by all the writers that the good Christian will make his opinions evident in that particular way. To be sure, as Rauschenbusch, Shailer Mathews, Francis Greenwood Peabody, and Ellwood insist, external changes are not enough; there must be a climatic change in the very temper of American life. All of them would agree with Peabody, however, that a retreat from the world is calamitous.

In speaking of Tolstoy, Peabody refers to the "hopeless impracticability" of his faith.

When, for example, an exalted nature like that of Tolstoi breaks away from social ties, scorning and rebuking modern civilization in the name of the Christian life, and at last, in the dark and cold of a Russian winter, abandons wife and family to secure for his last days Christian peace, what effect does this struggle for consistency make upon the modern mind?

His conclusion is that, like the charge at Balaklava, it was magnificent, but it was not war. "It did not win the battle of life: it ran away from that battle." [24] Peabody's conclusion is that the fundamental fallacy in the discouraging conceptions of Christian ethics which lead men to regard it as impracticable is the confusion "of the temporary, occasional, and incidental aspects of the Gospel with its universal, spiritual, and permanent message." [25] This applies to the eschatological interpretation of Schweitzer, but it also applies to the Christian quietism of Tolstoy.

. . . . To confuse Oriental imagery with universal principles, to single out a teaching of non-resistance as the core of the Gospel, to retreat from social obligations in the name of one who gladly shared them and was called a friend of wine-bibbers and publicans—all this, however heroic it may be, is not only an impracticable discipleship, but an historical perversion.[26]

Whatever might be the conclusions of other leaders of the Social Gospel in regard to the point of non-resistance, they would agree with Peabody that the life of the Christian is to be lived in the world, and that his social task is in helping to transform this present world into the Kingdom of God. And whether definitely worked out or not, it has been understood by most of the advocates of that view that the State plays a large part in this. After all, the repressions of society upon the freedom of individuals, whether in the economic or the political sphere, are not to be removed except by law. It is indeed true that the spirit of society is the principal thing, but certainly repressive laws must be replaced by nonrepressive laws. And unless Christians are willing to wait until every single man has been converted to the view they consider that of Jesus, it is necessary that laws should be passed which give to men the possibility of developing their personalities to the fullest extent. Those who have worked hardest for the Social Gospel have been willing to use the coercive power of the State to prevent employers from exploiting workmen, and to give proper opportunities for children and for minorities. They have thus, tacitly at least, accepted the police power of the State in the same way that the historic Church has accepted it. They have not believed, generally speaking, that the police power of the State can be invoked to make men good. But that power may be invoked to prevent evil.

There is here one distinction between the historic efforts of the Christian Church, as exemplified in the Middle Ages or in Geneva, and the social program of the proponents of the Social Gospel. In the Middle Ages and in Geneva, the Church as a social unit exercised its power either as correlative with the State or as over the State to bring about political changes. The outlook of the Social Gospel is nonecclesiastical. The Kingdom of God is much larger than the Church itself, and the Church no longer acts as an institution. Social changes are brought about by individuals influencing others to act in "the spirit of Christ." But the thing to be kept in mind is that the Social Gospel for its concrete exemplification in society demands the use of the State as an instrument in preventing evil and in enlarging the possibilities of human life.

It was inevitable that modern pacifism should stem out of the Social Gospel movement. This statement will, I think, be justified later; but it is not to deny the peace interests of millions of Christians who

203

never subscribed to the more extreme tenets of the social movement in the churches. Nor is there any question of denying that nonresistance was held as a doctrine by individual Christians and especially by the historic groups, such as the Quakers and the Mennonites, without any reference to the Social Gospel. One may even go further and remark that pacifism played little part in the teachings of the leaders of the Social Gospel movement in its beginning. Dr. Charles H. Hopkins, in his book *The Rise of the Social Gospel in American Protestantism, 1865–1915,* has one reference to "Pacifism" in his index, and that is to one page out of 327. But the development of pacifism after the World War was inevitable. The Social Gospel defined the Kingdom of God as the organization of humanity on earth according to the will of God. And a people who had wearied and sickened of war were quick to believe that here was the great obstacle to such an organization of mankind.

Chapter IX

MODERN PACIFISM

MODERN PACIFISM STEMS OUT OF THE SOCIAL GOS-
pel. "It is in this realm," wrote Visser 't Hooft, "that
the Social Gospel of the last years sounded its strongest notes." [1] The term "modern pacifism" has been
chosen deliberately, for it must be distinguished from
the historic Christian pacifism of Tertullian, of the
Waldenses, of the Mennonites and the Quakers. The
new pacifists partake of the virtues and of the de-
fects of the movement from which they come. As
has been said, the earlier phases of the Social Gospel
dealt little with pacifism, but after the first World
War this entered strongly into the thinking of leaders of the movement.

During the first World War pacifism was discussed along the lines familiar to the Church.
Everything that could well be said about this was
said in the journals of the time.[2] The shock of war
to peaceful and peace-loving people forced consideration again of the age-old question. Actually, the
first reaction of many leaders of the Social Gospel
movement when America finally entered the struggle
was that here at last was a genuine crusade for a
better world. No better illustration can be chosen
than the attitude of a distinguished American Christian who for several decades has been a great voice

205

especially to college students of America and of the world.

> I believed it was a war to end war [he wrote later], to protect womanhood, to destroy militarism and autocracy, and to make a new world "fit for heroes to live in"—a world of liberty, equality of opportunity and fraternity; a world of peace based on justice. . . . . It was a kind of holy crusade, a half-divine crucifixion of humanity for saving the world.[3]

And these beliefs are understandable in the light of the teachings which had become popular in America.

The central tenet of the Social Gospel was that the supreme task of Christianity is to Christianize the social order. Men like Rauschenbusch had labored nobly to eradicate injustice in economic and social life. But the success of such efforts depended upon a stable government, and especially upon a government in which the ultimate authority is in the people—in other words, a democracy. Therefore, whatever threatened democracy in the world threatened the success of the social mission of the Church. Moreover, war itself was the great enemy of the Church in the accomplishment of these ends. Like the modern businessman, the advocates of the Social Gospel required a peaceful and, to some extent at least, a democratic world to carry on his work. Although the religious leaders did not always recognize this, it was the supplanting of military by economic forces in the modern state which made possible the kind of social progress which has come to be regarded as the work of the Kingdom.

The long half-century between the close of the Civil War and the outbreak of the first World War had been a time of unparalleled opportunity for those who wished to devote themselves to social progress. The only interludes of international strife were the War with Spain and the disturbances in the Philippine Islands, short and of little moment as such things go. On the whole, so far as international relations are concerned, America, to borrow Chesterton's words,

> Lay in a patch of peace
> Like a dog in a patch of sun.

And it is against this background of peace and of the widespread preaching of the Social Gospel that one must understand the reaction of many American Christians to the first World War. To them the slogans, "to make the world safe for democracy," "the war to end war," denoted not simply a struggle born of desperate necessity to prevent the swamping of the little that man had accomplished in trying to live decently in a democratic and peaceful world, but a positive step forward toward Christianizing the social order. The soldiers sang about Tipperary and other less-edifying subjects, but in some minds there echoed the old song:

I have read a fiery gospel, writ in burnished rows of steel:
"As ye deal with my contemners, so with you my grace shall
    deal!"

This is not to say that only those who preached

207

a Social Gospel spoke in these terms, but it is to say that for many who subscribed to that gospel the war seemed the next logical step in the spread of Christian principles. Here was an Armageddon which men could understand: it was being fought for the possession of the earth in the name of the Lord. Only when this state of mind is understood can one appreciate the violent reaction which swept many churchmen after the war into loud renunciation of all wars.

The brave new world did not come. After the war a group of nations wrangled over the spoils. America herself refused to have anything to do with international efforts to maintain law and order; and, unconscious of the way in which her own technology was washing away her continental security, she rejected the League of Nations which her own President had fathered. A false prosperity beckoned men to bigger and better spending, and the Church had full coffers but a declining spiritual leadership.

The American leader referred to above will serve again to illustrate the way in which pacifism became a central conviction in the minds of many. After looking forward to a war that would end war, this leader realized that the end of the struggle had not brought the result for which the democracies had been fighting. "The war that was to end war," he wrote, "had started a score of smoldering conflagrations." And he summed up his impressions of the war to a group of students in words whose beginning is reminiscent of Augustine. "The saddest thing is not that some ten millions of our best young men are

208

dead, that the world is impoverished, victimized on
both sides by a distorted propaganda, embittered by
hate, rent by division, suspicion and fear. It is that
neither side seems to have learned the lessons of the
war." The statement begins like Augustine, "What
is the evil in war?" But the ending is different. Augustine had said that the real evil of war is not that
men die, but that hate and lust are loosed in men.
The American leader sees as the greatest evil of the
first World War that it did not end war: the Crusade
had failed.

The story continues in terms familiar to all who
have read the confessional literature of the Church.
There is one step yet to be taken before the final surrender is made. This comes at last. "Now, at last,
after ten long years, I have reached bedrock in my
conviction. I have found stable equilibrium in my
thought. I am finally done with war. I too, can
now say with that growing army of men and women
of good will in every land, 'No more war!' "

One cannot miss the moral earnestness of this
search for a "stable equilibrium," nor the obvious
sincerity of the writer in announcing the conviction
which he had reached. But neither the moral earnestness nor the sincerity should blind us to the fact that
the writer was moved not only by the horror of war,
but by the conviction that the war to end war had not
brought in a better world. The first World War
had not been the final stage of the Social Gospel.

The twenties were difficult for the Church. In
America there was unprecedented giving for building

209

churches and promotion of missionary work. But the atmosphere of the decade was bad for spiritual effort. Never was the country so dominated by devotion to "science." Those who sought to uphold the Church and her teachings found themselves constantly on the defensive, trying to defend a very much shortened line. It had been too long preached that the end of Christianity was to bring peace and security to man. Why, asked opponents, inject a moribund institution and a supernatural theology into a plain and simple effort? The social programs which the Church had fostered were being taken over by "specialists," who claimed to be able to do much better without the Church what the Church had taught them to do.

And the liberal branch of the Church in America, as well as elsewhere, was busy defending such of its theology as could be saved from the debacle. In the early twenties a collection of sermons published as the "best sermons" of the year was issued with an editorial introduction calling attention to the fact that each sermon asked a question. The editor did not say whether the questions were answered. The liberals found themselves fighting, on the one hand, the "Fundamentalists" and, on the other, the liberals who were outside—one does not say beyond—liberal Christianity. The tone of much of the learned world was that of a distinguished professor who said to his seminar: "When social work has taken over the charity of the Church and the psychologist has found a substitute in music and the arts for 'dim, cathedral light,' what is there left for the Church?"

In the social field, Christianity of the Social Gospel type found itself facing a new and stubborn foe in a jubilant Marxism. America, outside of certain intellectual circles, had paid little attention to Karl Marx until after the Russian Revolution. Then the country was filled with voices lauding the Communist experiment as the answer to man's long struggle for justice and for equal opportunity. In the 1900's it had seemed sufficient to waken the Church to social needs. Rauschenbusch, indeed, had believed that Christian Socialism is the way out. But right-wing, nonviolent Socialism had fallen into disrepute, and the left-wing sympathizers seemed realistic heirs to the future. At least they had a philosophy, an interpretation of history, and a program. If one contended that the end of the Church was to bring the Kingdom of God upon earth in a stable and just and Christian order, the Marxists could reply: "Here is a demonstrably quick way to exact from every man according to his ability, and to give to every man according to his needs."

The newer way seemed the quicker; and this is important in winning men in this world. In 1933, with the shadow of Hitler falling over Germany, Adolf Deissmann said to the writer that one must remember that both Nazism and Communism are apocalyptic movements. They offer men sudden ways of salvation. Accept us, they say, and we will give you what you desire. In the face of such alluring promises the old, slow way of evolutionary progress, the gradual Christianization of the world, seemed poor and fruitless.

It is against this background of the wreck of exuberant hopes and the challenge of other methods, that one must understand the rise by leaps and bounds of pacifist sentiment. Men of good will rejected the violence of the Communist, for they had seen the defeat of their plans by war. They would end war, not by the old, slow method of establishing international order, as men had worked long to build stable states with internal peace. One does not suggest that international peace seemed more easily obtainable than the solution of the intricate problems of international and social justice. But it was natural for men, shocked by war, to turn to the distinctive gospel, "No more war."

An interesting sidelight on the twenties in America is the amount of attention given to Tolstoy, St. Francis, and Gandhi. Two of them were of countries far removed from American knowledge, and the other was of a far-distant century. All were pacifist, according to the interpretation given them in much contemporary writing. It is illuminating to turn the pages of the United States Catalogue and of the indexes to periodical literature for this period. Books and a flood of magazine articles described the beliefs and techniques of these three men. Tolstoy was a dramatic figure, sleeping in his country home in a bare room and at last fleeing even the cheerless walls of his self-imposed cell to die on his way to retirement into the simplicity and peace he loved. St. Francis, seen across the centuries, was an apostle of nonresistance, although twentieth-century readers did not intend to begin where he began—with poverty. As for Gandhi, there was great attraction in what he had to say about soul force—such attraction that his admirers did not always remember that nonviolent resistance is also resistance.

It became popular to assume that the essence of Christian moral teaching had always been nonresistance. Not only those who had become pacifists, in the modern sense, but even scholars in no way sympathetic with the idea, wrote as if the Early Church had held tenaciously to this principle until it had been corrupted by delusions of military and civil grandeur. A scholar like Hobhouse could write that "the conception of a brotherhood of love based on the negation of self is demonstrably inadequate to the problem of reorganizing society and intelligently directing human effort. . . . ." And at the same time he could believe that it was in the matter of war that the failure of the Church is most conspicuous, for the Anabaptists and the Quakers, almost alone, had gone back to the primitive teachings of the gospel in regard to war.[4] In other words, nonresistance is absurd, but the Church ought to teach it.

At this point, we should remind ourselves again of the nature of Christian pacifism. It may seem too elementary for notice, but writers do not always show that they are aware that Christian pacifism, in its ordinary interpretation, means rejection of the right

213

of the Christian to take part in *any* war, on *Christian* grounds. Those who have convinced themselves that war is unreasonable and always futile may be right, but their intellectual conviction is not Christian pacifism. The records of the draft boards in the second World War will show that several people have been puzzled because they thought that the State's exemption of conscientious objectors from military service meant that whoever did not agree with the government as to this particular war should be exempted. But exemption on grounds of religious objections to war has never been taken as inclusive of those who simply disagree with the government. Neither does rejection of a particular war as unjustifiable qualify as Christian pacifism. The writer can remember when his own father denounced the Spanish-American War and refused to allow his eldest son to enlist. But this did not mean that the father was a pacifist. The Church has frequently held, as these pages testify, to the duty of the subject (or citizen) who does not feel satisfied that a particular war is just, to refuse to serve. This is not pacifism, but the inalienable right of a Christian man to follow his conscience. If his conscience comes into conflict with the powers that be, the Christian must suffer for it, if necessary. He cannot fall back upon exemption for conscientious objectors who renounce all wars as impossible to the Christian man.

The first point in which modern pacifism differs from that with which the Church has long been familiar is that the modern variety is less thorough-

214

going than the old. It is understood, let it be said again, that we are not here speaking of Mennonites and Quakers, although some of them have shifted their historic position. But the pacifist today is quite likely to admit coercion in restricted spheres. For example, Kirby Page believes that the police "do serve as a constructive and redemptive force in society, in spite of many miscarriages of justice and occasional misuse of power." Whether the arguments by which he justifies this discrimination between coercion within the State and coercion between states are valid is not here in question.

In the second place, nonresistance is urged by modern pacifists as a strategy. Again Kirby Page has revealing passages. In discussing the German invasion of Belgium (in the first World War), he asked: "But how could aggressive good will have freed the soil of German invaders?" Aggressive good will is not merely nonresistance, but, it must be kept in mind, is to follow and to involve absolute nonresistance. The two, as the pacifist himself insists, are bound up together. And how this is to work is set forth by Mr. Page: it is "by convincing the German people that they had no reason to fear invasion of their own land, and thereby depriving the militarists of their support and driving them out of control of the government." [5] How much fear the Germans in 1914 had of invasion from Belgium is beside the point. Nonresistance and aggressive good will are strategies to remove the invaders from the land, although Mr. Page admits that it might have taken a good while.

To the question, "What should a Christian in the United States do if our soil is actually invaded by a foreign army?" Mr. Page has this answer. "It is usually assumed that if it did occur only two alternatives would be open to us: (1) to resist the invader with an army and navy; (2) to lie down and do nothing. But surely there is a third possibility: resist the invaders by active good will expressed through appropriate channels." [6]

In view of the tragic events in this country since December 7, 1941, one does not care to dwell upon the burden which would have to be carried by the Christians who attempted this program. They might vindicate their integrity in the sight of God, but in the eyes of their fellows they would undoubtedly stand as those fifth-column traitors beside whom they would be working and whose ends they would be furthering. However, such mundane matters do not enter into the argument. Mr. Page was certain that such conduct on the part of Christian people would convince "the rank and file of people in the nation from which they come of our good will and in that way deprive the invaders of support from their home base." [7] How the armies and navies of the invader would be "deprived of support from their home base" Mr. Page does not say. In Japan and Germany, it would apparently have to be by revolution; but it would be German and Japanese blood shed in that case, and this may not count.

The naïveté of such a proposal, which could come only from a people so little acquainted with the blood and iron of totalitarian policies or the actualities of warfare as the Americans have been in the immediate past, can be left for debate by those to whom the questions of strategy are pertinent. So far as Christian pacifism is concerned, the problems of strategy for removing invaders are not in point. No twist of the sayings of Jesus or Paul can make them propose nonresistance or anything else as a strategy for removing armies from conquered lands. In the sayings of the gospel there is provision for the salvation of the individual opponent's soul, but this has nothing to do with plans of high commands, ecclesiastical or other, for dealing effectively with the enemy.

Some reference must be made to one occasional element in the discussions of modern pacifism, that of so-called nonviolent resistance. Reinhold Niebuhr has said all that needs to be said about this, and it is sufficient here to state that a technique for overcoming a superior force by a resistance that does not harm property or lives is still a technique for overcoming a superior force, and has little more relation to the teachings of Jesus than the techniques of war.[8] Certainly one cannot imagine Jesus giving his disciples lessons in psychology to prepare them for what Gregg calls "moral jiu-jitsu." [9] The popularity of Gandhi in America during the twenties is, of course, responsible for this strange turn to discussions about nonresistance. But nonviolent resistance, noncooperation, by whatever name called, is a technique to secure political power, to secure material possessions. To see in these a carrying out of our Lord's

217

counsels is to misread all that he said. He treated the ends which men seek—goods, power, worldly domination—as indifferent. If it is difficult for a modern man to think in those terms, the matter is not helped by presuming that these ends are all right if some means are used which translate force into other terms than guns and swords.

Another important distinction between modern pacifism and that known by the Church through the centuries is in the relation of the Christian to the State. Many Christian pacifists—Waldenses, Mennonites, Quakers, and others—recognized the State's duty to keep order, although they objected to the way that it was done. But they did not assume that the State's power should be used to bring in the Kingdom on earth. Only the apocalyptic sects, such as the Münster Anabaptists, could resort to force for this purpose, and they admitted the use of the sword in war as well as in peace. The historic Christian pacifist refused usually to take any part in government because this involved the use of the sword, which Paul said the ruler did not bear in vain. The pacifist sects were "content to set up the most perfect and unselfish individual life as a symbol of the Kingdom of God"; and they felt that they could do this only by "disavowing the political task and by freeing the individual of all responsibility for social justice." [10]

The modern pacifist, however, finds himself in a different position. Spurred by the belief that the purpose of Jesus was to establish the Kingdom of God

218

upon earth and by the conviction that this can be done by the gradual spreading of the Spirit of Christ, he has committed himself to the use of the State to help alleviate misery, to ensure justice, and to promote the general welfare. In doing so he willingly takes part in a coercive society, for these things can be done only through, in the end, the coercive power of the State. The modern pacifist draws the line only in protecting the State from external aggression. International lawlessness and injustice are without his sphere of interest.

It is replied at once that in war men are killed. If it is held that there must never under any circumstances be any taking of human life, the position is clear at any rate. Not only capital punishment, but any resistance unto death on the part of police must be ruled out. But it is argued that in war the innocent are killed. So they are. For a long time, in the evolution of society, the innocent suffered with the guilty in the preservation of internal order. We have gone a little way beyond that, although the innocent still suffer from crime and sometimes in the suppression of crime. But to have no international justice until some method is devised whereby only the guilty suffer is to postpone a decent world until our children's children have known death and suffering, perhaps even forever.

We are all guilty, we are told; so it is not meet that one nation should suffer. There is little need to argue about this. If the totalitarian State, with its oppression of religious and racial minorities, is no more to be blamed than a country that, with all its sins, has achieved more freedom than any other nation ever had, then moral judgment has abdicated. As a matter of fact, there is a sense in which every member of society is guilty of the criminal's acts. His environment may have been bad; his training may have been inadequate; his medical treatment may have been defective. But few believe that the criminal should go free because of this. And this raises the whole question of responsibility in the modern State. Until very recent times it made no difference what the individual subject thought about the policies of State. He had but two choices: to obey or to rebel. The advice of Christian teachers, that the Christian should obey his own conscience, takes on grim meaning when one remembers that during most of the history of the Church to follow one's conscience frequently meant death. But with the development of democratic processes, greater and greater responsibility rests with the individual citizen.

Has the citizen, therefore, the right to say that, because the government did not follow his advice, war has come; and, therefore, because the government ignored proper counsel, he is free of responsibility? What did the citizen do when the country failed to follow his advice? Did he withdraw from citizenship? Or did he continue to pay taxes, knowing that his money would be spent in preparation for war? Did he continue to vote, thereby acknowledging himself still a part of the body politic? It is possible that, during the last twenty years, many things could have been done by this country to lessen the chances of war with Japan. Unquestionably the Exclusion Act did not help feeling between the two countries. Many Christians and others protested against it. But, even if Japan did not plan war regardless of the Act, the Christian who continued a citizen of this country in spite of the actions taken against his advice accepted responsibility for the corporate act of his people. This does not, of course, mean that he must fight despite his own conscience; but it does mean that he cannot hold himself of all men guiltless for the acts of his government. He accepted the will of the majority, in fact if not in his mind.

If any man were always right, intellectually as well as morally, in his position on international affairs; if he made no mistakes as well as wished no evil; if when his vote was overridden he then withdrew from citizenship, paid no taxes, accepted no part in the country's life, he could honestly say that he had washed his hands of guilt. If not, with all others he must say: "This also is my act and my guilt."

As one looks back over the history of the Church, three facts are evident. The Church has always abhorred war. No good word is found among the great writers of the Church for the calamity, which they regarded as an evil like the plague. But the Church, in its main tradition, has always believed that man must live in society, and for this reason governments are instituted among men. In the words of the Apostle, "the powers that be are ordained of God"; and in many centuries the Christian continued to do all that he could to support that government, paying taxes or serving in civil or military life as might be necessary. The realistic thinkers of the Church knew that the judge and the soldier posed great problems for the Church, but they believed that a wise man would not shrink from his duties, even though those duties brought him into that darkness of which Augustine spoke. But even as they believed that human society required law and order within the nation, so they believed them required between nations. And generations of Christian thinkers gave their best thought to means for safeguarding that peace and order between national groups. To maintain this international law and order they recognized that the force necessary for internal order must also be used between groups. Mistakes were made—and will be made—but always the aim was international justice and, above all, the security of peace.

It is true that we are internationally at the stage where pioneer communities in America were when the six-shooter was the only law. To evolve out of such chaos an orderly society is a task at once difficult and dangerous. Yet until such international order is achieved there must be wars. To suppose, in the world as it now is, one nation or group of nations can achieve a democratic society unmolested by those whose interests and ambitions are thwarted, is to suppose that our shrunken world can remain half slave and half free. Of course, Christians can sanction

222

police force within nations but refuse to have anything to do with international justice until that far-off time when some Society of Nations can insure peace with a minimum of coercion. But when that good day comes, the generation which knows its glories will be indebted, in large part, to those who have struggled for such approximation of justice as was possible before the coming of Law.

There are many ways in which the Christians of other days differed from some of our contemporaries. They did not believe that the Kingdom of God was to be built upon earth. They welcomed a better world, and some of them worked for it. With their limitations, Thomas Aquinas and Calvin, each in his own way, did no little to lay down the laws of a Christian State. But all of them "looked for a city which hath foundations, whose builder and maker is God." They believed that death is the last enemy to be overcome, not that it is the only one, as a man might be inclined to believe if he were sure of a continuous, if slow, progress of society toward the Kingdom.

So for each man there is a choice which only he can make. It has been made clear in this book, I trust, that those who believe that it is sometimes better to die than to suffer some ills to befall one's country and one's children, that justice, relative as it always is, must be maintained between nations by force, have an ancient and honorable lineage. There is a multitude of witnesses, not stupid nor unchristian men, who have never glorified war, but who have accepted the necessities of an imperfect world and have not shrunk from the grim burdens of the social order. With them many of us believe that "if any one endures or thinks of wars without mental pain, his is a more miserable plight still, for he thinks himself happy because he has lost all human feeling." [11] With them, also, we believe that we must carry our part of the burden, and that there may be times when, as a judge or as a soldier, the Christian must act as it is meet and right for a Christian to do, "for human society, which he thinks it a wickedness to abandon, constrains and compels him to this duty." [12]

NOTES

ABBREVIATIONS

CSEL....*Corpus scriptorum ecclesiasticorum latinorum.* Edited by the Vienna Academy of Letters. Leipzig, 1866- .

MGP ....*Patrologiae cursus completus. Series Graeca.* Reprint. Paris, 1928.

MPL ....*Patrologiae cursus completus. Series Latina.* Paris, 1878-90.

WA.....*D. Martin Luther's Werke. Kritische Gesamtausgabe.* Edited by J. K. F. Knaake, G. Kawerau, E. Theile, and others, Weimar, 1883- .

INTRODUCTION

1. Nils Ehrenström, *Christian Faith and the Modern State* (Chicago: Willett, Clark & Co., 1937), will give the reader a very good resume of contemporary theories of the relations of Church and State with some sketch of the history. The bibliography given in this volume is very good for recent aspects of the question. Troeltsch's great work, frequently referred to below, is good for the history of the theory of Church and State and of the various Christian doctrines of the State. The notes to Troeltsch's volumes give full references to other studies, although chiefly European.

Chapter I

THE TESTIMONY OF JESUS

1. G. H. C. Macgregor, *The New Testament Basis of Pacifism* (London: James Clarke & Co., Ltd., pref. 1936), p. 10.

2. C. J. Cadoux, *The Early Church and the World* (Edinburgh: T. & T. Clark, 1925). This work is not altogether

without coloring from the author's pacifist convictions. Cf. review by J. F. Bethune-Baker, *The Journal of Theological Studies*, XXII (1921), 294-96. The references to Cadoux in the following pages are to be found in Part I, chap. v.

3. The reader who wishes to see the evidence for both sides of question should consult James Moffatt, art. "War," *Dictionary of the Apostolic Church*.

4. R. H. Charles, *A Critical History of the Doctrine of a Future Life* (2nd ed.; London: A. & C. Black, 1913), pp. 379 ff. For later summaries, see A. E. J. Rawlinson, *St. Mark* ("Westminister Commentaries"; 3rd ed.; London: Methuen & Co., Ltd., 1931), *ad loc.*; B. Harvie Branscomb, *The Gospel of Mark* ("The Moffatt New Testament Commentary"; New York and London: Harper & Bros., n. d.), *ad loc.* Bacon dates the section in Mark and Matthew after the Fall of Jerusalem. (Benjamin W. Bacon, *Studies in Matthew* [New York: Henry Holt & Co., 1930], p. 469.)

5. *Ecclesiastical History* iii. v. 3 (Edward Schwartz, ed., *Eusebius Werke* ["*Die griechische christlichen Schriftsteller*"; Leipzig, 1903], II, 196). Apparently Wellhausen and Loisy were the first to suggest that the words of Jesus concerning flight referred to the Fall of Jerusalem.

6. Cf. Hans Lietzmann, *Geschichte der alten Kirche* (Berlin and Leipzig, 1932), I, 185.

7. Charles Gore, *Jesus of Nazareth* (London: Thornton Butterworth, Ltd., 1929), p. 94.

8. Vladimir Simkhovitch, *Toward the Understanding of Jesus* (New York: The Macmillan Co., 1921).

9. Carl David Soule, in Edwin Prince Booth, ed., *New Testament Studies* (New York and Nashville: Abingdon-Cokesbury Press, 1942), p. 251. But elsewhere in the same chapter Mr. Soule recognizes the fanatical character of the Zealots.

10. William Fairweather, *The Backgrounds of the Gospel* (Edinburgh: T. & T. Clark, 1911), pp. 195-96.

11. R. Travers Herford, *The Pharisees* (New York: The Macmillan Co., 1924), pp. 187-88.

12. Professor Bacon summarizes the situation as follows: "Social conditions were probably much more galling to the ordinary peasant or artisan of Galilee in Jesus' time than political. . . . . The cry of the Zealot nationalist still availed to rouse the patriotic ardor of some, especially in rural Galilee; but their numbers dwindled as experience of the exchange from native war-lord to Roman governor taught the peasant farmer how slight was the alleviation of growing burdens of taxation and forced labor which any such exchange could be expected to bring. . . . . The longing for political freedom should not be overrated. . . . . We may probably conclude that the average fisherman, artisan, or peasant landholder of Galilee was ready to put up with such measure of peace and order as Roman government brought, if only he were permitted to answer according to his custom and ability the ever-pressing questions, What shall we eat and what shall we drink, and wherewithal shall we be clothed? Native justice was hardly an improvement on Roman." (*Op. cit.*, pp. 423-24.)

13. Cadoux, *op. cit.*, p. 43. I do not want to leave the impression that all that Cadoux has to say about Jesus' attitude toward war is contained in his discussion of this passage and the "specific instructions" quoted above. In the sections of his book in which he discusses Jesus' ethical teachings and his attitude toward the State, Cadoux has some pertinent and weighty arguments. I have confined myself to the specific passages because I am dealing here with the actual sayings of our Lord, not with discussions of the application of his ethical principles, and because of the importance that these sections have assumed in less critical writings.

14. *Jesus and Civil Government* (New York: George H. Doran Co., 1923), pp. 19 ff.

15. *Love in the New Testament* (New York: Richard R. Smith, Inc., 1930), pp. 118-19.

227

16. P. 10.
17. P. 60.
18. Soule, *op. cit.*, p. 248.
19. *Love in the New Testament*, p. 73.

Chapter II

FROM ST. PAUL TO CONSTANTINE

Hugo Grotius, in his great *De jure belli ac pacis* (1646), reviewed the patristic sayings about war. The work may still be used with profit to study the evidence of the Fathers. See the edition in the series "The Classics of International Law" (Oxford: Clarendon Press, 1925) II, 81 ff. Discussions of the attitude of the Early Church and of the Church in the Middle Ages, giving quotations from the sources, are to be found in John Eppstein, *The Catholic Tradition of the Law of Nations* (London: Burns, Oates & Washburne, Ltd., 1936); Alfred Vanderpol, *La doctrine scolastique du droit de guerre* (Paris, 1926).

Quotations from the Fathers are, wherever possible, from Alexander Roberts and James Donaldson, eds., *The Ante-Nicene Fathers* (10 vols.; New York: Charles Scribner's Sons, 1925); Philip Schaff, ed., *A Select Library of the Nicene and Post-Nicene Fathers* (14 vols.; New York: The Christian Literature Co., 1886-90); Philip Schaff and Henry Wace, eds., *idem*, second series (13 vols.; New York: The Christian Literature Co., 1890-98). References are given so that the quotations may be found both in the English translations and in editions of the sources.

1. C. J. Cadoux, *The Early Church*, p. 84.
2. *Annals* XV. 44. See L. H. Canfield, *The Early Persecutions of the Christians* ("Studies in History and Public Law," No. 136; New York: Columbia University Press, 1913), pp. 45-59.
3. On parallelisms between Emperor worship and Christianity, as well as on the wide extent of the imperial cult, see Adolf Deissmann, *Light from the Ancient East* (English trans.; London: Hodder & Stoughton, 1927), pp. 338 ff.

4. *"Die antirömische Stimmung der Juden hat wohl früh in der christlichen Gemeinde Widerhall gefunden und ist später schnell durch die Verfolgungen gewachsen: der Gegensatz zum Kaiserkult spielt dabei eine wesentliche Rolle: zugleich wirken chiliastische Gedanken ein, um das Christentum 'weltfremd' zumachen."* (Hans Lietzmann, *Einführung in die Textgeschichte der Paulusbriefe an die Römer* ["*Handbuch zum Neuen Testament*," 8; *vierte Auflage*; Tübingen, 1933], p. 111.)

5. Deissmann deliberately uses the plural "classes" to avoid suggesting the existence of a proletarian class in the Roman Empire. (*Op. cit.*, pp. 7-8.)

6. Ernst Troeltsch, *The Social Teaching of the Christian Churches* (English trans.; New York: The Macmillan Co., 1931), I, 80-81.

7. A. J. Carlyle thinks that there was an anarchical tendency in the Early Church similar to that which appeared later in the Anabaptists, and, from the same cause, a misinterpretation of the divinity of man. (*A History of Mediaeval Political Theory in the West* [Edinburgh and London: William Blackwood & Sons, Ltd., 1927], I, 93-97.)

8. C. J. Cadoux, *op. cit.*, pp. 88-89.

9. Cf. Wisdom 6:3. See Lietzmann, *An die Römer*, on Rom. 13:1-7.

10. Carlyle, *op. cit.*, I, 97-98.

11. C. H. Dodd, *The Epistle to the Romans* ("The Moffatt New Testament Commentary"; New York: Ray Long & Richard Smith, 1932), p. 201.

12. Cf. W. M. Ramsay, *The Church in the Roman Empire before A.D. 170* (New York: G. P. Putnam's Sons, 1893), pp. 314-15.

13. *To the Romans* 4, 5 (J. B. Lightfoot, *The Apostolic Fathers* [ed. and completed J. R. Harmer; London and New York: Macmillan & Co., 1891], pp. 121-22).

14. Chap. xxxix (MPG, vol. 6, col. 388*B*).

15. Chap. cx (MPG, vol. 6, col. 729*B*).

16. Adolf Harnack, *Militia Christi, die christliche Religion und der Soldatenstand in den ersten drei Jahrhunderten* (Tübingen, 1905), pp. 47-51. This is the standard work on the subject. Students should also consult: James Moffatt, art. "War," *Dictionary of the Apostolic Church;* Harnack, *The Mission and Expansion of Christianity in the First Three Centuries* (New York: G. P. Putnam's Sons, 1908), II, 52-64; A. C. McGiffert, "Christianity and War—a Historical Sketch," *American Journal of Theology,* XIX (1915), 323-45.

17. This letter, which was quoted by the Fathers and accepted by them as genuine, is given in *The Ante-Nicene Fathers,* I, 187. The letter has long been recognized as spurious.

18. *Apology* xlii (MPL, vol. 1, col. 491).

19. Chap. i (MPL, vol. 2, cols. 76-77).

20. *Ibid.*

21. *Militia Christi,* p. 67.

22. *Ibid.,* p. 117.

23. *Ibid.,* pp. 114-17. Harnack reprints the *Acts* of Marcellus and of Maximilianus in an appendix.

24. *First Epistle to the Corinthians* xxxvii (Lightfoot, *op. cit.,* p. 25).

25. *Exhortation to the Heathen* x (Otto Stählin, ed., *Clemens Alexandrinus* ["Die griechischen christlichen Schriftsteller"; Leipzig, 1909] I, 72). See James Moffatt, art. "War," *Dictionary of the Apostolic Church.*

26. *A Plea for the Christians* xxxv (MPG, vol. 6, cols. 968-69).

27. *Epistle to Donatus* 6 (MPL, vol. 4, col. 205*A*). Frequently Cyprian is referred to as a pacifist. Even Professor Moffatt ("War," *Dictionary of the Apostolic Church*) says that Cyprian is one of the writers who "explicitly oppose war." But Professor C. J. Cadoux rightly cannot agree with this. The latter thinks that Cyprian, because of his anti-secular bent, may possibly have agreed with Tertullian, but he says that Cyprian "nowhere—in the writings of his that have come down to us—had occasion to say in so many words

whether a Christian might or might not serve in the legions." (*Op. cit.*, pp. 581-82.) But the point is that Cyprian did have several occasions to express his mind on this subject, and did not. His most explicit statement, according to Cadoux, is in the treatise *On the Advantage of Patience* 14: "Adultery, fraud, manslaughter, are mortal crimes . . . . nor, after the Eucharist carried in it, is the hand spotted with sword and blood." (I hasten to say that the translation is from *The Ante-Nicene Fathers*. The last clause reads: "*nec post gestatam Eucharistiam manus gladio et cruore maculatur.*" [MPL, vol. 4, col. 651C]).

28. *Against the Heathen* i. 6 (CSEL, IV, 8). On Arnobius, see Pierre de Labriolle, *History and Literature of Christianity from Tertullian to Boethius* (English trans.; New York: Alfred A. Knopf, 1925), chap. iv.

29. *On Idolatry* xix (CSEL, XX, 53).

30. *Concerning the Crown* xi (MPL, vol. 2, cols. 91C-92).

31. *Ibid.*

32. *Annals* I. 35.

33. *On Idolatry* x (CSEL, XX, 39-41).

34. *Ibid.* xvii (pp. 50-51).

35. *Stromata* vii. 12 (*Clemens Alexandrinus*, III, 55).

36. *Against Celsus* v. xxxiii (Paul Koetschau, ed., *Origenes Werke* ["*Die griechischen christlichen Schriftsteller*"; Leipzig, 1899], II, 35).

37. *Ibid.* vii. xxvi (II, 176-78).

38. *Ibid.* viii. lxxiii (II, 290-91).

39. *Ibid.* viii. lxxv (II, 292). The phrase σύστημα πατρίδος is translated "national organization." I am indebted to Eppstein for calling attention to these quotations from Origen.

40. *Divine Institutes* vii. xxv (MPL, vol. 6, col. 813A).

41. *Ibid.* vi. xx (col. 708A). Professor Moffatt remarks that no early Christian writer is so Tolstoyan in his ethics as Lactantius, but that his proofs are drawn from humanitarian considerations and not, as those of Tertullian, from the New Testament. ("War," *Dictionary of the Apostolic Church*.)

Chapter III

THE CHURCH AFTER CONSTANTINE

1. T. R. Glover, *The Conflict of Religions in the Early Roman Empire* (8th ed.; London: Methuen & Co., Ltd., 1919), p. 343.

2. John T. McNeill, *Christian Hope for World Society* (Chicago: Willett, Clark & Co., 1937), p. 9.

3. Edward Rochie Hardy, Jr., *Militant in Earth: Twenty Centuries of the Spread of Christianity* (New York: Oxford University Press, 1940), p. 55.

4. Augustine, *Of the Morals of the Catholic Church* xx (MPL, vol. 32, col. 1327).

5. Augustine, *Sermons on New Testament Lessons*, sermon xxxi. 7 (MPL, sermon lxxxi, vol. 38, cols. 503-4).

6. *Ibid.*, sermon lxxv. 11 (MPL, sermon cxxv, vol. 38, col. 697).

7. Canon 3. See Karl Joseph Hefele, *Histoire des conciles*, ed. and trans. into French by Henri Leclercq (Paris, 1907-38), vol. I, 1, pp. 282-83.

8. *Against Heresies* v. 24 (MPG, vol. 7, col. 1187B).

9. See the references given by Lietzmann, *An die Römer*, pp. 40-41. Lietzmann says: "*Das alles sittliche Handeln die Befolgung der uns von der Natur eingepflanzten Gesetze sei und in der Gottheit wurzele, ist der Fundamentalsatz der stoïschen Ethik. . . . .*"

10. Dodd, *Epistle to the Romans*, p. 36.

11. *The City of God* xix. 15 (CSEL, XXXX, 400).

12. *Ibid.* (p. 401).

13. *Ibid.* Cf. Carlyle, *Mediaeval Political Theory in the West*, vol. I, part III, chap. 2.

14. *Ibid.* xix. 12 (p. 393).

15. *Ibid.* xix. 17 (p. 404).

16. See Étienne Gilson, *The Spirit of Mediaeval Philosophy* (New York: Charles Scribner's Sons, 1936), p. 475 n. 21, and the citations from Augustine given in this note.

17. *The New Schaff-Herzog Encyclopedia,* by S. M. Jackson and others (New York: Funk & Wagnalls, 1908-12), art. "War and Christian Service in War." But in the *Realencyklopädie für protestantische Theologie und Kirche,* ed. A. Hauck (3rd ed.; Leipzig, 1896-1913), art. *"Krieg,"* Burger makes Augustine's position clear. It looks as if Burger's article *"Krieg"* had been abbreviated thoughtlessly for the *Schaff-Herzog.*
18. *The City of God* iv. 4 (CSEL, XXXX, 166-67).
19. *Ibid.* xix. 7 (pp. 383-84).
20. *Ibid.* (p. 384).
21. *Epistola* xxv (MPL, vol. 16, col. 1084).
22. J. D. Mansi, *Sacrorum conciliorum collectio* (Florence and Venice, 1759-98), XX, 459. See Vanderpol, *op. cit.,* pp. 115 ff.
23. *The City of God* xix. 6 (CSEL, XXXX, 382-83). On the attitude of Augustine toward war, see T. S. K. Scott-Craig, *Christian Attitudes to War and Peace* (New York: Charles Scribner's Sons, 1938), pp. 50-84. Most of the relevant quotations are given by Vanderpol and Eppstein.
24. *Reply to Faustus* xxii. 75-76 (CSEL, XXV, 673-76).
25. Letter cxxxviii. 10-11 (CSEL, XXXXIIII, 134-37).
26. *Ibid.* 14 (pp. 139-40).
27. *Ibid.* (pp. 140-41).
28. *Reply to Faustus* xxii. 74 (CSEL, XXV, 672).
29. Letter clxxxix. 4, 6 (CSEL, LVII, 133, 135).
30. *Quaestionum in Heptateuchum Libri VII,* vi. x (CSEL, XXVIII [II], 428).
31. *Summa Theologica* II. xl. i. The translation is that of the Dominican Fathers, *The Summa Theologica of St. Thomas Aquinas,* literally translated by the Fathers of the English Dominican Province (22 vols.; London: Burns, Oates & Washburne, Ltd.; New York, Cincinnati: Benziger Brothers, 1920-37).
32. The text of Francisco de Vitoria, *On the Law of War,* is to be found in Ernest Nys, ed., *Francisci de Victoria De*

Indis et De jure belli relectiones (Washington: Carnegie Institution, 1917). A translation of *On the Law of War* is to be found on pp. 163-87. On Francisco de Vitoria, see Introduction to this volume by Ernest Nys, and James Brown Scott, *Francisco de Vitoria and His Law of Nations* (Oxford: Clarendon Press, 1934). The latter is a valuable discussion of the scholastic doctrine of Natural Law and of the State, and of the contribution of the Spanish school to International Law.

33. A French translation of Suárez' section, *De bello,* in his treatise, *De triplici virtute theologali,* is in Vanderpol, *op. cit.,* pp. 362-412.

Chapter IV

MONKS AND SECTARIES

1. Athanasius, *Life of Antony* 2 (MPG, vol. 26 [II], col. 841).
2. Cf. definition of Christian asceticism by E. Dublanchy, art. "Ascétisme," *Dictionnaire de théologie catholique,* ed. A. Vacant and E. Magenot (Paris, 1909-   ).
3. *Against Marcion* v. vii (CSEL, XXXXVII, 594); i. xxix (p. 330).
4. *On the Dress of Virgins* 3 (MPL, vol. 4, col. 443B).
5. Letter xxii. 20 (CSEL, LIV, 170-71).
6. *Of Holy Virginity* 27 (CSEL, XXXXI, 263-64).
7. On the theory of property in the Early Church, see Carlyle, *op. cit.,* vol. I, part III, chap. 12.
8. Letter cxxx. 14 (CSEL, LVI, 193).
9. Letter xxii. 33 (CSEL, LIV, 195-96).
10. Charles, Count de Montalembert, *The Monks of the West* (London: John C. Nimmo, 1896), I, 18 ff.
11. *Against Vigilantius* 16 (MPL, vol. 23, cols. 351C-52A).
12. Athanasius, *Life of Antony* 44 (MPG, vol. 26, col. 907B).
13. Chrysostom, *Homilies on the Gospel of St. Matthew* lxix. 3-4 (MPG, vol. 58, cols. 651-54).
14. Letter lxxxii. 10 (CSEL, LV, 117).

15. T. F. Crane, *The Exempla or Illustrative Stories from Sermones Vulgares of Jacques de Vitry* (London: pub. for the Folklore Society, 1890), Exempla cxvii, cxviii.

16. Quotations from the Rule are from Thatcher and MacNeal, *A Source Book for Mediaeval History* (New York: Charles Scribner's Sons, 1905). The Rule is also accessible in F. A. Gasquet, *The Rule of St. Benedict* (London: Chatto & Windus, 1925). A convenient edition of the text is S. *Benedicti regula monasticorum,* ed. Benno Lindebauer, O. S. B. (*"Florilegium patristicum,"* fasc. xvii; Bonn, 1928).

17. Chap. 53.

18. Chap. 67.

19. For the more recent phase, see G. G. Coulton, *Five Centuries of Religion* (Cambridge: The University Press, 1923), vol. I, appendix 8, pp. 458-64.

20. *Op. cit.,* I, 309.

21. Crane, *op. cit.,* Exemplum cxvi.

22. Letter lxvi. 8 (CSEL, LIV, 656).

23. *Of Holy Virginity* 14 (CSEL, XXXXI, 246-47).

24. *Summa* II. clxxxiv. 3.

25. *Ibid.* I. cviii. 4. Cf. E. Dublanchy, art. *"Conseils evangeliques,"* *Dictionnaire de théologie catholique.*

26. L. Duchesne, *Histoire ancienne de l'eglise* (Paris, 1910), II, 521.

27. The epistles of Gregory are bk. iii, ep. lxv (MPL, vol. 77, cols. 662-63); bk. viii, ep. v (cols. 909-10). There is an account of the controversy in F. H. Dudden, *Gregory the Great, His Place in History and Thought* (London and New York: Longmans, Green & Co., 1905), II, 181-85.

28. *Summa* II. clxxxviii. 3. The quotation from Ambrose is from *Duties of the Clergy* i. xxvii (MPL, vol. 16, col. 66B).

29. H. B. Workman, *The Evolution of the Monastic Ideal* (London, 1918), pp. 277-78.

30. *Of the Work of Monks* 28 (CSEL, XXXXI, 574).

31. Paul Sabatier, *Life of St. Francis of Assisi* (English trans.; New York: Charles Scribner's Sons, 1922), p. 69.

32. *The Little Flowers of St. Francis* 8. This has often been translated. A convenient edition is that in Everyman's Library. Cf. Sabatier, *op. cit.*, pp. 138-39.

33. See Sabatier, *op. cit.*, pp. 267 ff.

34. Paul Sabatier, ed., *Le speculum perfectionis ou mémoires de frère Léon* (Manchester: University Press, 1928), p. 5. (There is an English translation in the Everyman's Library volume mentioned in note 32.) Cf. the statement in the Testament of St. Francis (4): *Et illi qui veniebant ad recipiendum vitam* [*istam*], *omnia quae habere poterant dabant pauperibus, et erant contenti tunica una, et foris repetiata, cum cingulo et bractris.*

35. *Ibid.*, pp. 12-16.

36. See Sabatier, *Life of St. Francis*, p. 97, and sources referred to in the note.

37. *Ibid.*, p. 126.

38. *Speculum perfectionis*, p. 40.

39. Sabatier, *Life of St. Francis*, pp. 80-81.

40. *Sermon against Auxentius* 2 (MPL, vol. 16, col. 1050B).

41. *Duties of the Clergy* i. xxxvi (MPL, vol. 16, col. 84A).

42. *Ibid.* i. l. (cols. 103B-4A).

43. Troeltsch, *The Social Teaching of the Christian Churches*, I, 331 ff.

44. H. C. Lea, *A History of the Inquisition of the Middle Ages* (3 vols.; New York: Harper & Bros., 1888) is still an indispensable book for the history of medieval heresy. With the exception of this there is not much in English on the Cathari. There is a useful article by F. Vernet, *"Cathares," Dictionnaire de théologie catholique*, and one by J. Guiraud, *Dictionnaire d'histoire et de géographie ecclésiastiques*, ed. A. Baudrillart and others (Paris, 1912-). These articles have extended bibliographies.

45. *Anecdotes historiques, légendes et apologues d'Étienne de Bourbon*, ed. Lecoy de La Marche (Paris, 1877), pp. 290, 292. Lea, *op. cit.*, gives the best account in English of the Waldenses. See also H. C. Vedder, "Origin and Early Teach-

ings of the Waldenses, According to the Roman Catholic Writers of the Thirteenth Century," in *American Journal of Theology*, IV (1900), 465-89; C. H. Haskins, *Studies in Mediaeval Culture* (Oxford: Clarendon Press, 1929), chap. XI, "The Heresy of Echard the Baker of Rheims."

46. *Anecdotes historiques*, pp. 290, 292.

47. Bernard Gui, *Practica inquisitionis heretice pravitatis* v. ii. The standard edition of Gui is by C. Douais (Paris, 1886); but there is a convenient edition of Book V, with a French translation, by G. Mollat (2 vols.; Paris, 1926-27). The section of the *Practica* devoted to the Waldenses contains a good deal of material from Étienne de Bourbon, who was himself an inquisitor.

48. H. B. Workman, *John Wyclif* (Oxford: Clarendon Press, 1926), II, 27, 28, 303.

49. Troeltsch, *op. cit.*, I, 362.

50. Workman, *op. cit.*, II, 396 f.

Chapter V

THE REFORMATION CHURCHES

Well-known works of Luther are cited from the familiar English editions; other references are to the Weimar edition of his works, or to special editions. Calvin's *Institutes* are quoted from a standard American edition.

1. For Luther's views on monasticism, see James Mackinnon, *Luther and the Reformation* (London and New York: Longmans, Green & Co., 1929), III, 22 ff.

2. *Ibid.*, III, 32.

3. Cf. Albrecht Ritschl, *Justification and Reconciliation* (English trans., ed. H. R. Mackintosh and A. B. Macaulay; Edinburgh: T. & T. Clark, 1900), pp. 647-48.

4. Philip Schaff, ed. and trans., *The Creeds of the Evangelical Protestant Churches* (London: Hodder & Stoughton, 1877), pp. 50-51.

5. *Ibid.*, p. 56.

6. *Ibid.*, p. 57.

7. *Ibid.*

8. Henry Wace and C. A. Buchheim, trans. and eds., *Luther's Primary Works together with his Shorter and Larger Catechisms* (London: Hodder & Stoughton, 1896), p. 362.

9. *Ermahung zum Frieden auf die zwölf Artikel der Bauerschaft in Schwaben* (1525; WA, vol. 18, p. 310). See Troeltsch, *op. cit.*, II, 866.

10. George Buchwald, ed., *Predigten D. Martin Luthers* (Gütersloh, 1925), I, 22 ff. Luther's two-Kingdom theory has resulted practically in the moral dualism with which he charged the Catholic Church. See, e.g., Nils Ehrenström, *op. cit.*, pp. 69-70.

11. Luther, *Von weltlicher Obrigkeit, wie weit man ihr Gehorsam sei* (1523; WA, vol. 11, p. 259); quoted by Troeltsch, *op. cit.*, II, 846. I have followed Troeltsch in his exposition of Luther's views on the State, as they are set forth in this treatise and in the *Auslegung der Bergpredigt* (1532; WA, vol. 32, pp. 299-544 [*Wochenpredigten über Matth. 5–7*]). For a criticism of Troeltsch's interpretation see Emil Brunner, *The Divine Imperative* (Eng. trans.; New York: The Macmillan Co., 1937), p. 681. On Luther's view of the State, see also: *Der 82 Psalm ausgelegt* (1530; WA, vol. 31 [I], pp. 182[189]-218); *Ob Kriegsleute auch in seligem Stande sein können* (1526; WA, vol. 19, pp. 616[623]-66); *Vom Kriege wider die Türken* (1528; WA, vol. 30 [II]), pp. 81[107]-148).

12. Wace and Buchheim, *op. cit.*, pp. 60-61.

13. Schaff, *The Creeds of the Evangelical Protestant Churches*, pp. 16-17.

14. See tractate, *Vom Kriege wider die Türken*.

15. William Hazlitt, ed. and trans., *The Table Talk of Martin Luther* ("Bohn's Standard Library"; London: George Bell & Sons, 1884), pp. 333-34.

16. For a convenient survey of Luther's opinions on war, see Scott-Craig, *Christian Attitudes to War and Peace*, chap. iv.

Wesley and Modern Religion (Nashville: Cokesbury Press, 1936).

4. The view that Wesley reacted against Protestantism is set forth by Maximin Piette, *La réaction wesléyenne dans l'évolution protestante* (Brussels, 1925). This has been translated into English. That Wesley reaffirmed the position of the Reformers was argued by the late Professor George Croft Cell, *The Rediscovery of John Wesley* (New York: Henry Holt & Co., 1935). See H. B. Workman, "The Place of Methodism in the Catholic Church," in *A New History of Methodism* (2 vols.; London: Hodder & Stoughton, 1909).

5. "Advice to the People Called Methodists with Regard to Dress," *Works*, XI, 466 ff.

6. *Works*, VIII, 185.

7. Sermon xliv, "The Use of Money," Edward Sugden, ed., *Wesley's Standard Sermons* (London: Epworth Press, 1921), II, 311-27.

8. *Works*, XI, 196-98.

9. *Works*, XI, 154 f.

10. *Explanatory Notes on the New Testament, ad loc.*

11. Sermon xlviii, *Standard Sermons*, II, 416.

12. See his "A Word to a Freeholder," *Works*, vol. XI; Warner, *op. cit.*, chap. iv; Taylor, *op. cit.*, pp. 24 ff.

13. "The Doctrine of Original Sin," *Works*, IX, 221-22.

14. *Letters*, III, 165.

15. *Ibid.* The poems are in *The Poetical Works of John and Charles Wesley* (London, 1870), vol. VI.

16. *Letters*, VI, 143.

17. *The Poetical Works of John and Charles Wesley*, VI, 184-86.

18. J. L. and Barbara Hammond, *Lord Shaftesbury* (2nd ed., London, 1923), p. 153.

19. Art. "Shaftesbury, Seventh Earl of." For Shaftesbury's life and work, see, in addition to the life by the Hammonds, Edwin Hodder, *The Life and Work of the Seventh Earl of*

Shaftesbury (3 vols.; London: Cassell & Co., Ltd., 1887); Bready, *op. cit.*

20. See pertinent remarks by Taylor, *op. cit.*, pp. 92 ff.

21. Bready, *op cit.*, p. 40. See chap. iv for a discussion of Shaftesbury's political principles and for the quotations on war given below.

22. Hodder, *op. cit.*, III, 16.

23. *Ibid.*, III, 458 ff.

24. Bready, *op. cit.*, p. 121. For an account of Shaftesbury's activities and attitudes during the Crimean War, see Hodder, *op. cit.*, vol. III, chap. xxii.

25. Hodder, *op. cit.*, II, 485.

Chapter VIII

THE SOCIAL GOSPEL

1. W. A. Visser 't Hooft, *The Backgrounds of the Social Gospel in America* (Haarlem, 1928), pp. 38-39. Visser 't Hooft's study is the most thoroughgoing theological criticism yet made of the Social Gospel. Although he is sometimes misled by the complexities of the American scene and is influenced in his conclusions by his Reformation theology, the study cannot be passed over by those who would understand recent American religious developments.

2. Vernon P. Bodein, "Walter Rauschenbusch," in *Religion in Life*, Summer, 1937.

3. *Christian Realism* (New York: Charles Scribner's Sons, 1941), p. 80.

4. Charles Howard Hopkins, *The Rise of the Social Gospel in America, 1865-1915* (New Haven: Yale University Press, 1940), p. 99.

5. Visser 't Hooft, *op. cit.*, p. 16.

6. George Santayana, *Character and Opinion in the United States* (New York: Charles Scribner's Sons, 1920), pp. 14-15.

7. Elmer Ellis, *Mr. Dooley's America* (New York: Alfred A. Knopf, 1941), p. 176.
8. *A Theology for the Social Gospel* (New York: The Macmillan Co., 1917), p. 219n.
9. *The Social Teachings of Jesus* (New York: The Macmillan Co., 1917), pp. 13-14.
10. *The Reconstruction of Religion* (New York: The Macmillan Co., 1922), p. 83n.
11. *Which Way Religion?* (New York: The Macmillan Co., 1931), p. 118.
12. *Ibid.*, pp. 120-21.
13. For a brief discussion of developments in the New Testament field, see the essay by my colleague, Professor Fred Daniel Gealy, "The 'Ipsissima Verba' or the 'Ipsissimus Spiritus,'" in Booth, ed., *New Testament Studies*.
14. Rauschenbusch, *op. cit.*, p. 142.
15. Mathews, *op. cit.*, p. 54.
16. Ellwood, *op. cit.*, p. 184.
17. Rauschenbusch, *op. cit.*, p. 144.
18. *Ibid.*, p. 178.
19. *Ibid.*, pp. 142-43.
20. Ellwood, *op. cit.*, p. 185.
21. *Ibid.*, pp. 217-18.
22. *Ibid.*, p. 246.
23. Ward, *op. cit.*, p. 218.
24. *The Christian Life in the Modern World* (New York: The Macmillan Co., 1916), pp. 16-17.
25. *Ibid.*, p. 23.
26. *Ibid.*, p. 26.

Chapter IX

MODERN PACIFISM

1. Visser 't Hooft, *The Backgrounds of the Social Gospel in America*, pp. 55-56.
2. *The Constructive Quarterly*, vol. II, had two articles, one

by Mgr. Battifol, "The Catholic Church and War," and one by H. T. Hodgkin, "The Church and War," setting forth the Catholic and the Quaker positions respectively. Some other articles were: P. Gavan Duffy, "War and the Christian Ethic," *International Journal of Ethics*, XXVII, 219 ff.; Donald W. Fisher, "War and the Christian Religion," *International Journal of Ethics*, XXVIII, 107 ff.; John M. Mecklin, "The War and the Dilemma of the Christian Ethic," *American Journal of Theology*, XXIII, 14 ff.

3. I have not given the reference for this and other statements of this particular writer because I am informed that he has abandoned his position of absolute pacifism. I have kept the statements, however, because they are typical and because they were repeated in writing and in public address to thousands of American college students during the twenties and thirties.

4. L. T. Hobhouse, *Morals in Evolution* (4th ed.; London: Chapman and Hall, 1923), p. 524; *Encyclopaedia of the Social Sciences*, art. "Christianity."

5. Sherwood Eddy and Kirby Page, *The Abolition of War* (New York: George H. Doran Co., 1924), p. 183.

6. *Ibid.*, p. 186.

7. *Ibid.*, p. 187.

8. *Christianity and Power Politics* (New York: Charles Scribner's Sons, 1940), pp. 10-11. The essay "Why the Church Is Not Pacifist" in this volume is the strongest statement of the historic position of the Church to be found in a few pages.

9. Richard B. Gregg, *The Power of Non-Violence* (Philadelphia: J. B. Lippincott, 1934), chap. II, "Moral Jiu-Jitsu."

10. Niebuhr, *op. cit.*, p. 5.

11. Augustine, *The City of God* xix. 7 (CSEL, XXXX, 384).

12. *Ibid.* xix. 6 (p. 382).

INDEX

Albigenses; *see* Cathari
Ambrose, 77, 111, 118-19
Anabaptists, 140, 147, 148-52, 163, 213, 218
Andrew, 21
Anthony, 97
Antichrist, 21
Apocalypse, The Little, 20-23
Apocalyptic literature, 21, 28
Aquinas, Thomas, 85-87, 109, 111, 223
Arnobius, 59-60
Asceticism, 97-98, 167
Athenagoras, 58-59
Audland, John, 162
Augsburg Confession, 128
Augustine, 72, 74-85, 101-2, 109, 112-13, 139, 145
Authority in religion, 15

Baptists, 151, 152, 162-63
Baptists, General, 155
Barclay, Robert, 156, 157
Bax, E. Belfort, 150
Baxter, Richard, 141-44
Benedict, Rule of, 105-6
Bennett, John C., 185
Bible, interpretation of, 16, 17-18, 80, 112-13, 124, 126, 131, 139, 147, 149, 193-96
Biblical criticism in America, 16, 193-97
Bourbon, Étienne de, 123, 124
Braithwaite, William C., 161
Bready, J. Wesley, 179
Bryan, William Jennings, 192
Buddhism, 97
Bullinger, Heinrich, 150

Burger, Karl, 76
Cadoux, A. T., 30
Cadoux, C. J., 19, 20, 23, 25, 26, 30, 32, 33, 34, 35, 42, 227
Calvin, 135-40, 145, 147, 223
Cathari, 121-23
Celibacy, 99-102, 109, 118-19
Celsus, 60, 63, 64
Charles, R. H. 21
Chesterton, Gilbert K., 207
Choisy, Eugene, 137-38
Church of England, Articles of, 141
Civil office, Christians and, 44, 62-63, 133, 160-61
Clement of Alexandria, 57-58, 63
Clement of Rome, 57
Communism, 211, 212
Constantine, 11, 69-71
Cornelius, 60
Coulton, G. G., 106
Councils: Arles, 72; Third Lateran, 123; Fourth Lateran, 123; Winchester, 77-78
Courts of law, Christians and, 47-48, 66-67, 150, 171-72
Cromwell, Oliver, 145
Cyprian, 59, 230-31

Deissmann, Adolf, 211
Denck, Hans, 149
Dodd, C. H., 48
Domitian, 44
Donatists, 119

Ellwood, Charles A., 195, 197, 198, 199-200, 201
End of World, 21, 39, 42, 46, 53
Epicureans, 47

247